YOU'RE A HOOKER, THEN

For Val, Roddy and Ross

YOU'RE A HOOKER, THEN

AN AUTOBIOGRAPHY

COLIN DEANS

MAINSTREAM
PUBLISHING

First published in Great Britain in 1987 by
MAINSTREAM PUBLISHING COMPANY (EDINBURGH) LTD
7 Albany Street
Edinburgh EH1 3UG

ISBN 1 85158 079 4

British Library Cataloguing in Publication Data

Deans, Colin
     You're a hooker, then : an autobiography.
     1. Deans, Colin   2. Rugby football players
     ——Great Britain——Biography
     I. Title
     796.33'3'0924   GV944.9.D/

     ISBN 1-85158-079-4

PHOTOGRAPHY ACKNOWLEDGEMENTS: Bob Thomas, Chris
Thau, George Ashton, James Galloway, Mike Brett, Ian Southern, Ian
Brand, Ian Rutherford.

Typeset in 11 point Baskerville by Pulse Origination, Edinburgh.
Printed in Great Britain by Billing & Sons, Worcester.

Contents

(Courtesy: George Ashton)

Introduction

SCOTLAND'S RUGBY 'D DAY'

6 JUNE, 1987. It was undoubtedly the most important day in my
rugby life, in the team's life and in that of Scottish rugby. We Scots
were thousands of miles away from home in New Zealand but we
knew a whole nation was behind us, that millions would be getting
up in the wee sma' hours to cheer us on in homes and clubhouses.
I got out of bed, had a quick shower, then I went round the
bedrooms of all the boys hyping them up. They didn't really need
that but it had dawned on me that this was the anniversary of 'D
day' when determined Allied soldiers, including a lot of Scots
laddies, had stormed the beaches of Normandy. I told the lads to
make this our rugby 'D day' . . . the day we beat the All Blacks.

The bus to take us to the ground at Lancaster Park in
Christchurch, where we had played the French two weeks before,
eventually drew up outside our hotel and we got on board. The
driver switched on a tape of the Corries with all the auld Scots
songs. I felt a lump in my throat but also I felt about ten feet tall.
This was my 52nd cap for Scotland — equalling the record — and I
wanted to lead the boys to a famous victory. My thoughts turned to
my Border town of Hawick and I wanted so much to make the folks
there, in particular my wife Val, my laddies Roddy and Ross and
my mum, proud of us all.

7

Conditions were perfect for the game. Sure the ground was a wee bit hard in places but I reckoned we could cope with that. The big Scots contingent with their flags and their singing were all set to cheer us on. It was simply marvellous to be involved in the whole thing.

In the dressing room after the team picture had been taken I looked around at the lads. We had sweated together, we had been drenched together, we had drunk together and I felt that nothing applied so aptly to the group, even if it was written by an Englishman, than those famous lines in *Henry V* before Agincourt which go, "We few, we happy few, we band of brothers". But enough of sentiment. It was time to go out on the pitch and get on with the job.

Once there, the New Zealanders performed their traditional Haka which is designed to frighten the pants off the opposition. But most of the boys had been around for a bit and the only new cap in the team, Derek 'Styx' Turnbull, was a Hawick man and they don't frighten easily. Anyway we didn't even look at the Haka performance. We Scots formed ourselves into a circle, linking arms and yelled encouragement at each other so that not only did we not see, we couldn't hear the singing that goes with the Haka. I was a bit annoyed at a New Zealand TV man who stuck his microphone into the middle of our circle, but that's showbiz over there.

I had won the toss and elected to kick off.

From that drop out the All Blacks gained possession. Sadly for us that set the trend of the game. I had thought they might be weak in the scrums but was soon proved wrong. From the first scrum we were under intense pressure and that was to go on for the full 80 minutes. We did play pretty well at the line-out but the New Zealand team's commitment and professional finishing make them very hard to beat anywhere.

I was quite pleased that we held our own in the first-half, although we were on the defending side quite a bit. When we did win quality possession we put the Blacks under pressure but I admit there wasn't much of that. Good tackling by the boys kept the score down and at the interval New Zealand led only by 9-3 with Grant Fox kicking three penalty goals to one by Gavin Hastings. Obviously the crowd of around 40,000 — the highest for any of the tournament games — had divided loyalties. Many of them had Scots blood in their veins but they were at the end of the day New Zealanders so we didn't get the backing we had against the other teams we had taken on. In fact the stadium was pretty quiet all that first-half and I suspect it was because the New Zealand Press boys had warned that Scotland had the personnel and the skill to inflict a shock defeat on the All Blacks. It was the first time I had seen the home crowd wavering in their expectation of an All Blacks win. At the break all I could do was to say what the boys already knew — that we must get more quality possession. We were desperate for points and ready to gamble, but the All Blacks forwards were being used well and the first real killer blow came when Alan Whetton crossed for a try. Then, with time running out, John Gallagher crossed for another try. With Fox kicking well the final tally against us was 30-3.

So our World Cup campaign had come to a sad end. I had been proud of the way the Scots kept on tackling those big, powerful All Black forwards and I think we deserved a little more than our three points. However full marks to New Zealand who played well and deserved to win. We had nothing like the control we had in our previous three games.

I and the rest of the lads were shattered by the time the final whistle went. Back in the dressing room, to say the team was deflated would be an understatement. I went round each one of them thanking them for their efforts in this particular match and also for everything they had done in the previous couple of months. As Derrick Grant once said: "If you are going to bow, you might as well bow to the highest mountain." That is what we had done that afternoon.

It had been an abrasive game. In the first-half Iain Milne, who had been carrying a calf muscle injury, was trampled over by the whole New Zealand pack when he went down, and Iain Paxton got a nasty head gash when caught by an errant All Black boot. There was one punch-up and all in all I found the opposition pretty niggly during the whole match. For the first time I remember when playing the Blacks there were sarcastic remarks made by their players to us — John Kirwan, one of the culprits, told us, "Enjoy your trip home, boys", long before the end of play. Indeed, much to my surprise and dismay, I must say I've never played against such an arrogant side, especially in the second-half.

You have to put a brave face on things and I had 90 minutes of Press and TV interviews before grabbing a quick shower and getting along to the after-match function. Here I made my last World Cup speech, expressing thanks to all those who had made this a tour to remember and not of course forgetting the Blacks who I thought must go all the way. At the dinner I was sitting beside Andy Dalton who was really the All Blacks captain but had been hampered by injury and had not been able to play in the opening games. Andy, a great friend of mine, told me he had been fit to play against us and he was really sick about not having been chosen. I think the Blacks needed an old head like Andy's to lead their young side and I'm positive with him around they would have shown a great deal more discipline.

Of the All Blacks we encountered I reckon Wayne Shelford, their No.8, most impressed me. I think he was the forward of the tournament. He looked like he was enjoying himself, even when he was causing you uncomfortable moments. The front row of the pack was also good, with prop Steve McDowell particularly strong, while the team have an up-and-coming star in Michael Jones who still shows a bit of rawness but is definitely one for the future. Behind the pack scrum-half David Kirk who was the stand-in captain had an easy job, while his stand-off Grant Fox merely kicked — which, to give him his due, he did remarkably consistently. If we had been able to pressure him however I think he would have broken. But we didn't get the chance. The All Blacks stuck fast to their traditional pressure game which can be boring, but it does bring results. In all the circumstances we had done none too badly in keeping the try score against us down to two. At any rate Andy and I had a good crack before saying our goodbyes. I then joined my lads, who were perking up by now. It was about 3 a.m. before the party broke up.

Next morning, Sunday 7 June, we came down for breakfast to find the irrepressible Bear, Iain Milne, had collected some champagne, so we had Buck's Fizz with our meal. Then we all got together to present the management and coaches with silver engraved tankards for which the boys had pitched in, and I got one myself from The Bear. Afterwards we watched television and saw France beat Fiji and Australia account for Ireland. I felt a bit sorry for Fiji who kept running at their illustrious opponents while Ireland struck too late to save their match. Following dinner I had a very early night and watched TV in my room along with David Sole, who was sharing with me, before dropping off.

Andy Dalton and Colin Deans at the World Cup Dinner: get off your knees, Dalton (Courtesy: Chris Thau)

On the Monday I phoned Val and she sounded a bit depressed. All I wanted to do now was to get home and forget about rugby for a while. I was physically and mentally drained and I don't think anyone really realised what a demanding tour this had been, coming on top of a tough international season at home. We were due to make a one night stop-off in Los Angeles but Bob Munro, the team manager, was hoping to extend it to two. Personally all I wanted was to see my family as quickly as possible. Before we left for the airport I had a visit from a distant relative, Jock Dawson, and I spent some time with him and his wife while he talked about my mum's side of the family.

At last we took off and found the Irish team were sharing the same flight. There was no escape. Dave Irwin tracked me down and made me sit, and drink of course, with some of his team-mates. It was a ten-hour flight to our re-fuelling stop at Honolulu but it seemed to pass very quickly. Another seven hours to Los Angeles where we landed to find, because of the international date-line, that in terms of local time we were still in Monday and had touched down earlier than we had left New Zealand. It was the first time I'd experienced two Mondays in one day and it inspired Finlay Calder to sing the inevitable *I don't like Mondays*.

We found we would be staying two nights, partly to let the boys pay a visit to the famous Disneyland. At dinner that night we were issued with 20-dollar tickets to use there, courtesy of the SRU. It was a very nice gesture and I'm sure Bob Munro and Bill Hogg must have worked hard to get the hierarchy back home to agree. But I was glad for the boys who deserved a little reward for all their efforts, and proud of the SRU for providing it.

Next morning I checked it really was Tuesday — even in Los Angeles — and went down to breakfast. I consider myself a fair trencherman but I couldn't do justice to the huge mound of food which included pancakes, waffles, eggs and bacon. Then the team made a short monorail trip to Disneyland from the hotel.

We each bought a hat in the Mad Hatter's Shop and at one time were in the haunted house where I reckon we scared half the ghosts. We had a good time relaxing after all the hard work and the only trouble was the queues for the main attractions, sometimes causing delays of up to an hour.

Next morning we had our passports to hand in for our flight to Heathrow and we took off in the afternoon. During the ten-hour journey I had a chat with Derrick Grant about how things might have been different if we had beaten the French instead of just drawing. "If" is a word that crops up often in rugby circles, but only after the event is over.

On arrival at London, both Roy Laidlaw and I had a spot of bother when going for our plane to Edinburgh. We each had bought toy Winchester guns for our boys but the Customs people took them away, putting them in the charge of the pilot for the short flight. They explained that this was a precaution in case any passenger spotted them, believed they were the real thing and started a panic.

The plane touched down exactly on time at Edinburgh and we were back to where we had left some weeks previously — empty-handed. It was a sad thought but we cheered up as we went down the stairs to a barrage of TV cameras and spotted our wives and families. Val was looking marvellous after her holiday and the boys seemed glad to see me. We were soon on the way home but the journey was taking its effect and while I tried to stay awake to play with the boys I soon crashed out on my bed. It was to be next morning before I felt like a dad again, taking Roddy to school.

Looking back on this first World Cup I think the Scots boys provided more than their fair share of the spectacle. We'd had a pretty good international championship but I knew there was more to come from the team and I had hoped we would come of age by beating the All Blacks. No side can have given more in the training paddock and the whole squad mixed well. I felt desperately sorry for the "dirt trackers" — the boys not selected for the side and who didn't get a game during the tour. They had to train just as hard if not more so, if possible, as the picked teams, in case they were wanted. They were also the guys who got up early, who visited schools and hospitals and appeared at social functions on Scotland's behalf, and who were expected to celebrate with the triumphant team as if they had played. I admired them immensely. Not one of them moaned, not one shirked his duty. A fellow like Roger Baird, who is a British Lion, didn't even get a seat on the bench. Norrie Rowan, an experienced campaigner, did manage one game when The Bear was injured but Jeremy Richardson, one of our up-and-coming young forwards, had to settle for the experience, from which I'm sure he'll benefit.

The World Cup on the pitch was a success for us. It showed new boys Richard Cramb, Derek Turnbull, Alan Tait and Greig Oliver what life was like at the top, helping promote the greatest sport in the world. Some of the games we played in I felt were the most exciting of the tournament. To me the World Cup was a definite success. It was well run and very well managed by our tour manager Bob Munro who was a fantastic ambassador for the SRU. It was a tournament and a team with which I was proud to be involved, in a side which was easy to captain.

I think it was a fitting end to my personal playing career. A career which has meant living out of a hold-all for 17 years. But I'll always love rugby and I cherish the friendships I have made all over the world and which I hope to continue making wherever the oval ball is king.

Chapter 1

YOU'RE A HOOKER, THEN

IT WAS hardly the most flattering of welcomes to the great game of rugby. I was a lad of around nine at the time and had gone down to play in a trial for my local Trinity Primary School. The voice of P.E. teacher Bill McLaren, whose Border accent was to become familiar to rugby's television followers all over the world, boomed over the park: "Hey you, tubby. What's your name?"

Shyly, I replied, "Colin Deans, sir."

"Is your faither Peter?" queried Bill.

"Yes, sir."

"You're a hooker, then."

So Bill and fate both decreed that once I reached senior status my destination was in the middle of the front row of the pack, although I did earlier play at times as a prop and thoroughly enjoyed it.

I have a bit of a reputation for being quick around the field and for that I must thank my mother, Isobel. She was born in Argentina but came to Scotland early on and settled in Hawick where she became the school athletics champion, specialising in sprinting.

Although most people outside the Borders think of the big Highland Games such as Braemar as the main sprinting areas, in fact there are many such meetings in this part of the world. When I became a teenager I competed in lots of them and the tradition of rugby players taking part continues very much to this day. I found the competitive nature of running gave me more confidence in stretching my legs on the rugby field.

I was never pushed in any particular direction as a child but as my mother was so keen on athletics and my dad Peter hooked for Hawick it was only natural that I should take an interest in sport. Strangely enough, while my older brother Stuart plays on the wing for one of the town's junior clubs, my younger brother Cameron has no sporting affiliations at all. I sometimes think my mother would have been better pleased if Stuart and I had stuck to running for I'm sure she hated cleaning our rugby kit which was invariably filthy after a training session. But she always turned us out immaculately before we took the field and I even remember that she used to put a crease in our shorts.

My dad was known to everyone in Hawick and I confess, to this day, even when Scotland has won an international in which I've played, some old worthy will come up to me and say bluntly, "Ye're no as good as your faither was." I must say I agree, for my dad's commitment to rugby was intense. I hope some of his dedication has rubbed off on me. He was never a man to lavish praise, taking the view that if any one of his sons wanted to play rugby and enjoyed it as much as he had then that was reward enough. It's a sensible attitude to take and one that I intend following with my own boys Roddy, eight, and Ross, four. At the moment Roddy is soccer-daft but there's still plenty of time for him to see the light.

I played a bit of soccer myself from the time I was about 13 until I was 15 and the way that came about was a bit unusual. I had been training with the rest of the boys at rugby alongside my good friend Raymond Corbett, who was a scrum-half and who played in that role for the senior side when he grew up. I can't recall us doing anything wrong but suddenly one of the P.E. teachers, Ernie Murray, turned to Raymond and me, saying, "You'll never make rugby players." That really hurt, I can tell you. So for a while after that we concentrated on soccer. I was mostly put in goal but it was good fun and I recall we raised a five-a-side team which went in for a competition. To our great surprise we won.

You can learn from any experience and certainly soccer helps any budding rugby player with ball control. There are quite a few of the boys who have made or would have made just as good footballers as rugby men. Take David Johnston, for instance. He played a season for Heart of Midlothian before returning to Watsonians and Scotland. And my favourite football story concerns Ian McCrae, the Gordonians and Scotland scrum-half. Ian was so good that the manager of a Highland football team asked if he would sign professional forms to play for them. "Sure," said Ian, "as long as I get Saturday afternoons off to play rugby."

Despite my brief acquaintance with the round ball game, rugby was always my sport. This was only natural in a town where wearing the green jersey of Hawick is the supreme honour.

Visits to Murrayfield to see Scotland in action were the highlights of my year when I was a boy. At the time my dad was President of Hawick Wanderers and a bus was always hired to take the team into the Capital. It was magic for a wee Border boy to be sitting with the players. Then, on the way home it was a ritual that we stopped at the Black Bull Hotel in Lauder, where the menu was always the same — a mixed grill. I don't mind admitting I like my food and this was really living it up, eating like a king and listening to the big lads discussing the finer points of the game.

My most vivid memory of those early international visits was the famous ordering-off incident involving the great All Black forward Colin 'Pine Tree' Meads back in December 1967 when I was 12 years old. I remember this huge, six feet four inches forward, head bowed, trudging off the pitch on the loneliest walk a player can take. Years later I checked up on what had happened. Irish referee Kevin Kelleher had given Meads a warning earlier in the game and when the big fellow lashed out with his boot three minutes from the end of the match as Scotland's famous fly-half David Chisholm got his hands on the ball there was nothing else the referee could do, having decided that it was dangerous play, but send Meads off. It was a great pity, for the All Blacks, who won the match 14-3, were a wonderful side to watch. That ordering-off was certainly a big sensation at the time when violence was never associated with the game.

As for myself, I resumed playing rugby with Hawick Wanderers when I was around 15. I see Ernie Murray now and again when I pass through his town of Haddington and he still looks a bit sheepish about having made the remark that I'd never make a player. But in fact I probably owe Ernie a vote of thanks, for his view made me that much more determined to reach the top.

Before that happened, of course, I had a long apprenticeship to serve. Even before I was playing at the most junior level I was very proud to be a ball boy at some of our local semi-junior games. The big boys who actually played were my heroes and even the under-18s I regarded with awe.

It seemed that everyone who was able-bodied played rugby in those days and every spare bit of grass in Hawick was put into use as a pitch. I remember one was right alongside the Teviot River. Of course every time the ball was kicked into touch it invariably landed in the Teviot. It was fine in the early part of the season when it was still warm and as ball boy I quite enjoyed jumping into the river to retrieve the ball. But it was a different story when the winter weather took hold. One solution was to get a pole with a net attached to fish the ball out. I became quite adept at this and I reckon that's where I developed an early love of fishing which I now find an ideal way of relaxing.

The team finally moved up-market to a better pitch but again the Teviot posed a threat. This time, when conversion kicks were taken they had a nasty habit of soaring over the bar and landing with a splash. I remember one particular game when a brand new ball was being used and the inevitable happened. A kick was taken and the ball duly landed in the river which was in spate. A family friend of my dad's offered me two shillings to get it safely ashore. In those days two shillings was a heck of a lot of money. Aside from that it was pretty much a matter of life or death to rescue the ball . . . if I didn't manage it I could see myself being sacked as ball boy and that would have been humiliation indeed. I scrambled along the river bank following the ball until I reached the salmon cauld. I waded in and eventually, soaked to the skin, got the ball and ran all the way back to the pitch. By this time the game had ended and all the players had gone, but I'm glad to say I still got my two bob.

That's what I like about living in the Borders. If people give a promise they'll keep it. And while outsiders may think Borderers are clannish they really are very human. You're one of a family.

I think I can illustrate this by recalling that when my maternal grandmother died, my dad, as President, was with the Wanderers on their Tuesday training stint. My mother was naturally upset and I was detailed to go and break the news. When I got into the

Later days: fishing for things other than rugby balls. (Courtesy: Bob Thomas)

Wanderers' dressing room and saw my dad I just broke down and cried. The whole team came over to try and cheer me up. I was still a wee boy then and despite my grief I felt warm and comforted.

On a cheerier note may I boast about the fact that whereas most rugby players and other sportsmen have one nickname I can lay claim to two? My first unofficial name came when I had left school and started playing for Hawick Wanderers, one of two very fine semi-junior clubs who are not only good on their own but act as feeders to the senior team. Anyway, at the time I carried a bit of puppy fat and my brother Stuart made the jibe: "You look just like a bean." From then on I was called Beano — nothing to do with the comic magazine, I assure you! When I moved up to the senior side Ian Barnes, the famous lock forward who also turned out for Scotland seven times, was a member of the team. Not hearing the pronunciation correctly and knowing my surname was Deans, he started to call me Dino. Now, nobody argues with a guy the size of Barney so the second nickname has stuck. I've been called a few other things in my time but, what the heck . . . as long as the selectors remembered my real name and kept asking me to turn out for Scotland that was good enough for me.

Borders rugby, even at the junior stage, is based on hard training. It was said that when Grand Slam coach Jim Telfer had finished with an international squad at a training session the actual game — even against the French or the Welsh — was easy and I can assure you that the current Scottish coach, Derrick Grant, is also no slouch in making his charges sweat. Both, I sometimes think, must have been script-writers for Churchill when he wrote his famous blood, sweat and toil speech. However my first memories of tough training go away back to the time when I started playing for Hawick Wanderers.

We used to change in the Hut, on the Weensland-Jedburgh road outside the town. It was very near a steep hill called Miller's Knowes which became famous locally because it was rumoured that Hughie McLeod, later to become the world-renowned prop, used to put on his clogs and run up the hill at six o'clock in the morning when no one was around. I don't honestly know if that was the case, for even in those days Hughie was too much of a god-like figure for me to have the impertinence to ask him. But certainly he was always super-fit and it paid off in the top rugby circles for him as he won no fewer than 40 caps.

Anyway, we young lads in the Wanderers team maybe didn't run up the hill but we certainly worked hard. There were no namby-pamby things like proper dressing rooms or a bath in the Hut, so we used to try and grab a few inches of space in which to change. Then we ran all the way through the town up to the top of the public park where we carried out our training. I reckon it must be about one-and-a-half to two miles in all so by the time we reached there we'd done a pretty fair stint already.

Our trainer at the time was a man with a famous name, Jim Aitken. Of course he wasn't the Jim who in 1984 was captain of the Grand Slam team. This particular Jim played for the Harlequins and had had a few games for the senior Hawick side. He was a kid at heart and enjoyed running around as much as we youngsters did.

In between the two seasons I played for Wanderers I kept fit by playing football. On top of that Raymond and I used to go road-running, sometimes as often as three times a week, so I really never got out of the training groove. The result was that when it came to team selection time I had a big advantage over lots of the lads who had taken a break during the summer and were just starting to build up their fitness.

When I was first chosen for Wanderers I was a prop, then I was moved to No.8 where I managed to score quite a few tries. At one time I was even picked at centre but I didn't actually play because of injury. Otherwise you might have been looking at another Jim Renwick!

We had a pretty good team in those days although we didn't have any of the trappings of a successful club, such as our own clubhouse. But we were very lucky because the patrons of the Queen's Head pub in the High Street adopted us. After matches we'd go in there for a pint or two and if the police came in we'd disappear into the toilet until they'd gone. It was pretty well frowned upon that semi-junior players should have a pint but it's all part and parcel of the game and I can't remember anyone going over the score. Mind you, if you wanted to keep playing you daren't overdo it, for word would soon go round the town and you'd find yourself dropped from whichever team you played for.

I progressed gradually from semi-junior rugby with the Wanderers to junior rugby, which was a big step up, with Hawick Trades. I remember there was a slim-looking prop in the team at the time called Norman Pender who was destined to play for Scotland in due course. We had a pretty good side and if my memory serves me correctly we scored over 1,000 points in my first season with the Trades. But I'll always have a soft spot for Wanderers and for the good friends in the Queen's Head who helped us when we were laddies. I was glad to be able to donate a set of international jerseys to the pub once I made it to the top.

Someone else I'll remember with gratitude was Netta Young who owned the Turf Hotel at Darvel and who took the Trades side under her wing. There was always a bite to eat and a pint or two on the house whenever any of the boys gathered there. I'm sorry to say she died recently but I'm sure all of us who benefited from her hospitality will remember her with affection.

My first real taste of the big time, I suppose, was when the Trades went to Glasgow for a seven-a-side tournament. We played in five very hard rounds but were narrowly beaten in the final. The winners received a cup and medals but all we got was a "thank you" for turning up. I was very disappointed but once the bus stopped at the Turf Hotel and Netta took us in for a meal and a drink my spirits lifted again.

In fact it was following the success of the Trades seven winning the South District Rugby Union tournament in April 1973 that my first real meeting with the girl who was later to become my wife took place. And of course it came about because of a rugby occasion.

Our greatest fan, Netta, was in the habit of laying on a dinner dance at the end of the season and despite the three-hour bus journey we all were keen to attend. My trouble was that I didn't have a girl to ask to the affair. Team-mate Colin Turnbull, now my brother-in-law, suggested I ask his wife's sister, Val. I had known her at school and of course we had bumped into each other after leaving — Hawick isn't such a big place — but I had never really spoken to her. Screwing up my courage I asked if she'd like to come with me. Actually I think she was more interested in the dance and the dinner than in my company! At any rate she agreed and the busload of players, officials, wives and girlfriends left Hawick on the Friday evening. Once we did get to the hotel I didn't exactly endear myself by doing what was considered the macho thing, along with most of the young lads, and spending my time propping up the bar having the odd pint and, of course, chatting away about rugby.

I don't think Val was all that pleased but at least as the bus was coming into Hawick about six in the morning — not the most exotic time — I managed to steal a kiss. We didn't make any arrangements to meet again but met by chance that same night. Our romance took off from there.

Chapter 2

EARLY WORM — LATE PLAYERS

RUGBY has dominated my life. I have a lot of important dates to remember, like being picked for my first cap, the captaincy of Scotland and later the British Lions. But the foundations for these honours were laid much earlier and I remember those days just as vividly.

My first game for the Trades was on 16 December 1972 when we beat Selkirk 79-4. I was picked for the first trial for the big team, Hawick — known all over Scotland as the Greens — at the start of season 1973/74.

What a line-up of talent we had in those days! Alastair Cranston and Jim Renwick were the dazzling duo of centres. Cranston would crash through the proverbial brick wall if the occasion demanded. And what can you say about Renwick? He was simply superb, with one of the most exciting side-steps in the business and a puckish sense of humour. I remember he once said to the great Andy Irvine of Heriot's and Scotland fame, "Shake my hand now, Andy. It's the only time you'll lay a finger on me in this game." Others around at the time were Colin Telfer, a very gifted stand-off, who was later to become Scotland's coach, prop Norman Pender and lock Alan Tomes. I thought Alan a bit unlucky in that he had to wait a season longer than me to get into the Greens but from then on our club careers ran in tandem.

Hawick Trades R.F.C. 1972/73.
L-R Back: R. Broatch, H. Graham, P. Coltman, A. Hogg, K. Douglas, N. Pender,
D. Aitchison, A. Taylor. L-R Front: C. Deans, R. White, T. Turnbull, C. Thomson,
B. Lauder, J. Auchenleck, D. Semple.

I came through the first trial with flying colours thanks to all the hard training I had been doing during the summer and I blessed the persistence of Raymond and some of my other friends who had insisted we keep up our gruelling fitness programme when it would have been so much more pleasant to relax in the summer.

In the second trial I was in the Possibles rather than the Probables team and faced a tough opponent in Billy Murray. My confidence was high however. I had a good day against him, and I thought I might be in with a chance. Mind you, even in something as important to all the lads as the trial there was still room for a bit of kidology. Winger Ian Chalmers and flanker Brian Hegarty, I remember, were the best of pals off the field. But they were playing for opposite sides in the trial. Chalmers, a speed merchant, broke away on a marvellous run and with his last side-step left his old mate Brian standing. Immediately Brian shouted, "You're in touch, Chalmers." That caused Ian to stop, although he was nowhere near the touch line and Hegarty came trundling up and thumped him to the ground. "I was just kidding you," he grinned. It wasn't cricket — or rugby come to that — and certainly not gentlemanly conduct, but it did lighten the tension.

YOU'RE A HOOKER, THEN

Some things are serious, however, and poor Val learned quickly what it would take to be a rugby player's girlfriend. On the Friday before the trial we were invited to Brian Lauder's wedding dance. Brian was a very good scrum-half who had just signed for a Rugby League side. His bride was a pal of Val's, so naturally we had to attend but I sat drinking Coke and fidgeting as my mind was on my big test the following day. Early on Val, knowing how important the match was to me, said, "Let's make our excuses and leave." I think I knew then she was the girl for me.

At the time of the second trial my father's sister, who lived in Blackpool but was married to a former Hawick stalwart, was on a visit. On the Sunday night my dad took her to the rugby club for a drink and they bumped into Robin Charters, then a Hawick selector and now of course convenor of the Scottish national selectors. My father explained that his sister, who was of course as daft on rugby as the rest of the family, was going home next day and asked if she could go back with good news of her nephew's progress. Robin confirmed that I had been chosen. But neither my aunt nor my father let out the secret and it was not until the team was officially announced on the Tuesday that I knew I was to make my debut for THE side.

The night before the match, which was a friendly against Ballymena, I don't think I slept a wink. When I got up, eating breakfast was the last thing on my mind despite my normally healthy appetite. As usual my father came to the rescue. He whipped up a raw egg, some sugar and a spot of brandy and, having swallowed that, I felt my nerves settle.

Once the game started of course everything fell into place. The local Press were kind to me, recording that I won four strikes against the head, and had made an encouraging first appearance. Hawick won by 26-15, with Jim Renwick in terrific form, and avenged a previous season's defeat by the Irishmen. I'll always remember the date — 1 September 1973 — not only because of my debut with the Greens but also because it was the first time I'd come up against Willie John McBride. Little did I know that ten years later I would be regarding the legendary Irish forward in anything but a friendly manner!

Most sportsmen I've found are superstitious about something or other and I'm no exception. I always use the same dressing room peg following that win over Ballymena and while I don't claim to

1st season with Hawick.

have been successful in every match since then, I'd feel upset if I had to use an unfamiliar peg.

Milestones in my first season with the Greens were the holiday game against Heriot's F.P. at Goldenacre on 22 September 1973, my first game on the sacred turf of Murrayfield against Edinburgh Wanderers on 6 October that year, and my first televised match appearance versus Gala on 28 October. I took a lot of ribbing following the Heriot's match because the programme listed me as C. Beans and that took a lot of living down. The Murrayfield match, though, gave me a real thrill — one which I get every time I play there of course. At the time Wanderers used to play on the international ground quite frequently as they were right next door and their landlords were the Scottish Rugby Union. I also remember the Gala game vividly because it marked the start of my friendship with Gordon Dickson, the Gala No.8 who played that day.

Friendship between a Hawick and a Gala man is as rare as that between a Boer and an ANC member. But Gordon and I have been great buddies over the years. I literally fell at his feet during the game. What happened was that I was going all out to strike the ball

27

and in desperation tried to use both feet at once. The Gala pack surged forward and my legs were trapped. So I had to release my hold on my props and fell to the ground where of course I was trampled on by the forwards' feet until I eventually landed up with Gordon looming over me. He had the decency not to add to my pain and humiliation at finding myself in such a spot and side-stepped me to let me get up and get on with the game which we eventually won 9-6.

The year 1974 started off on a high note when we had a convincing victory over Heriot's F.P. in the traditional New Year's Day fixture. Renwick, just starting his tremendously successful career, was in spectacular form and was largely responsible for the win. But the honours went also to Jim Scott, a six feet seven inches forward who was built in proportion to his height. For some unknown reason Jim suddenly emerged on the right wing and probably to his own amazement was given the ball. Off he went trundling 50 yards to score a great try. There was a big crowd in the stand at Mansfield Park that day and, as one man, they stood up to give him a cheer.

The year saw me scoring my first try for Hawick in a game against Kelso. It was a pretty soft effort, I admit. The stand-off miskicked and fortunately my reflexes were pretty sharp at the time and I just had to gather the kick and go over for the try. But the highlight of 1974 was the fact that Hawick won the first official Division One league title — not without a great deal of effort, I may add. The championship was up for grabs when we met our old friends Heriot's on 23 February. A win was needed for the outright title. I remember going over the line in injury time, with the score tied at 18-18. I honestly don't know what happened. I remember going down to ground the ball and suddenly it was out of my hands.

That draw left us with a play-off against West of Scotland who had a very powerful side at the time. It was a midweek match which attracted the biggest crowd I'd played before up until then — around 8,000 to 9,000 people. In the end we were beaten 13-9 but still won the title on points differential. Later that year the team were given a civic reception and I recall that amongst the guests present was Bill Connon, now the SRU President.

I remember 1974 with a great deal of affection. I chalked up what were to me some memorable firsts. That included my first game for the South Under-21 and my first tour. I'm glad to say that the South team beat Northumberland Under-21 at Newcastle when players like John Rutherford, Keith Robertson, Gordon Dickson and Roy Laidlaw — all destined to wear the blue jersey of Scotland — were in our ranks. I enjoyed that, but even more so that first tour to Coventry and Bath around the end of March 1974.

We went down 27-18 in our initial game against Coventry but at least I had the satisfaction of scoring a try. On the following day, a Sunday, we travelled by coach to Bath and stopped off for a bite to eat at a wayside pub. Big Norman Pender was in cracking form and was keeping the boys in stitches with some of his jokes as we sat outside in the sun with pints in our hands. So busy was Norman in regaling us with his tales that he didn't spot one of the boys, Bruce White, who was a farmer, digging up an extremely large worm. As Norman put down his pint to emphasise a point in the story he was telling, Bruce swiftly dropped the worm into his glass. You can imagine that Norman was highly gratified to see everyone rolling around laughing at one of his jokes. But he wasn't exactly smiling himself when he got to the bottom of his pint and spat out the dregs which included one half-drunk worm.

When we did get to Bath we booked into our hotel and everyone was told to have an early night in preparation for the next day's game. Dutifully some of the older lads like Jim Renwick said to Robin Charters who was in charge of the party, "Well, good night, Robin, see you in the morning." Hardly had they disappeared upstairs than Robin was outside the door of the hotel showing a turn of foot of which even Renwick would have been proud, followed by we younger players who had just been about to obey orders. Within seconds Charters was round the back of the hotel waiting to pounce on poor Jim and some of the old sweats who were clambering down the fire escape intent on going for a drink in the town. "Dae you think," uttered Charters, "that I came up the Clyde on a banana skin? Get to bed now." They did, we did, and we beat Bath narrowly the next day.

Later that year, in June I think it was, I was amongst some of the Under-21 players invited by the Scottish Rugby Union to attend the national coaching course. Looking back, we were pretty well used as guinea pigs for the ideas of coaches from all over the country, but it was still a big thrill to be asked up to Edinburgh where the course was held, then at Edinburgh University's Pollock

Halls and nowadays at the Riccarton Campus of Heriot-Watt University. Amongst the coaches taking part that particular term were such famous names as Bill Dickinson, who was Scotland's first official coach, or rather, adviser to the captain, as it was quaintly put when he was appointed, Ian Cosgrove and Jim Telfer.

But my most vivid recollection of that weekend was a game which took place as part of the course on the Saturday afternoon. My opposite number at hooker was John Shedden. He seemed to fade from the rugby scene pretty rapidly but he was a tremendous hooker and he certainly took me to the cleaners in that particular match. I learned a lot from Shedden in that brief encounter and also later on in the season from that much under-rated hooker Quintin Dunlop who played for West of Scotland.

Hawick have never found West an easy side to beat, particularly away from home, and I remember we went down to them on a Burnbrae pitch which was nowhere as good to play on as it is nowadays. After the game Dunlop came into the clubhouse wearing a pair of yellow slacks which, together with the official black blazer, red jersey and red and yellow club tie looked pretty garish to a quietly dressed bunch of Border boys. That was until Gordon Brown, the Lions lock, turned up with a pair of SCARLET trousers on.

In this season also I had my biggest representative chance to date when picked for the Scottish Border Club, in essence the South team, and we beat Durham County in that particular fixture. Then came selection for the full South team against Glasgow. Our coach at the time was Jim Telfer and we had literally no time together to train. Jim did his best with us by putting us through our paces for a full three hours on the night before the match. During the game I was paid a back-handed compliment by Hugh McHardy, who was scrum-half for the Glaswegians. He complained to me that he was feeling sore, physically, because I was charging down on him. I just thought to myself, "I must be doing OK if I'm getting on to him so quickly." There's no sentiment in business — if it's rugby business.

My next big step up the ladder was playing for the Scotland Under-21 side against the British Post Office, a game which we won by 13-11. I met up then with Gerry McGuinness, who was later to become a Scotland prop and who nowadays works for me. So I made a good friend as well as furthering my rugby experience on that occasion.

Another chap with whom I got friendly then was Ron Wilson who played for London Scottish and who captained the Under-21 team that day. I recall he turned up at the ground driving a nifty little sports car and with a nifty-looking girlfriend in the passenger seat. A typical city slicker, was my immediate reaction. But later, particularly on tour, I got to know Ron very well and he was magnificent company, a really good guy.

Being a member of such a famous club as Hawick teaches you not only humility — surrounded as you are by such good players, year in and year out — but also ambition. The first time I really looked ahead to the next stepping stone after club and district rugby was when we played Glasgow High on 8 March 1975. We won and took the championship. I sat down then to work out my rugby future and although it may have been a bit presumptuous at the time I wrote down that I wanted to play for both Scotland and the British Lions. It all seemed a bit far off then.

I was encouraged later that month in our game against Gala, always a tough fixture. I managed to score two tries. One was almost entirely due to our full-back and I had little to do but make for the line and touch down. The other, however, gave me great satisfaction and belief in myself. It started from about the halfway line from a line-out. I kicked round their winger, beat the full-back and simply hurled myself at the line. As one of the Press boys recalled later, it seemed more like Dixie Dean than Colin Deans going to ground. The reason I was so pleased with the score was that it showed me I was on the path I'd set myself — to burst through quickly from the front of the line-out and make my speed tell.

My first introduction to the international scene was when I was picked for the Scottish Rugby Union President's VII to take part in a Belfast tournament celebrating the centenary of the Irish Rugby Union. The President at the time was the late Charlie Drummond, the ex-Melrose and Scotland stalwart who was an extremely popular figure not only in the Borders but everywhere he went in the rugby world. We players were taken up to Glasgow in preparation for an early morning flight — around seven o'clock — the next day. I don't know why, but if there's an awkward hour to take off you can bet your boots that's the plane rugby men will be on. But there was no danger of our sleeping in on this occasion. For Charlie and his pal Jimmy Johnston had attended the Hawick dinner the previous night and arrived around 5 a.m. They caught the plane with us, looking as fresh as daisies.

Scotland didn't win the tournament but it was a great thing to be involved at this level. After the tournament, and naturally as we were in Ireland, we ordered up pints of Guinness. The dark frothy brew was going down a treat when suddenly the barman appeared and without a word took our glasses away. "Why?" we asked. "Sorry lads," he said, looking a bit sheepish, "the Guinness I served you is off."

I don't think I've drunk a pint of the stuff since.

Chapter 3

THE GREEN MACHINE

THERE has been much admiration, sometimes envy, of the way 'The Green Machine', as Hawick rugby club is known, grinds on, mostly successfully. As one of the 15 players privileged to take part in this success on most Saturdays, I'd like to say thank you to the backroom boys who make it all possible.

First of all there's the largely forgotten groundsman. Without a decent pitch to play on there would be no rugby at all. Then there's the committee who guide the fortunes of the club. Some of course are better than others, but by and large we in Hawick have been blessed with committee men who are as keen as the players to keep Border rugby, particularly of course Hawick rugby, to the fore.

Perhaps the most influential men nowadays are the coaches. They are an integral part of the game and it seems strange to my generation to think back to the era when coaching was frowned upon. There have been three coaches during the past decade who stick in my memory. But my No.1 choice must be Derrick Grant who nowadays is the man behind the scenes in Scotland's preparations for international fixtures.

I'm not ashamed to admit that Derrick, when I first came under his wing at Mansfield Park, instilled fear into me. I had heard so much about this martinet. Mind you, in those days Derrick was such a dedicated athlete and so determined on getting the best out of his charges that you might have called him blinkered. He was, and is, a man who instantly commands respect. Let me give you an example of how highly he is regarded in Hawick. When he was playing and coaching he always used one particular peg in the dressing room. Now he has moved on to greater things. But that peg always remains unused — as though the club is waiting for Derrick to return as a player.

A lot of folk used to consider us unlucky to have to train under such a demanding coach. Personally I'm more grateful than I can say to him. He pushed me — and the others — to the limit of exhaustion, then demanded more. He was, if you like, my guru in the jungle of international rugby. Even as I was equalling Jim Renwick's record as the most-capped rugby Scot he was trying to help me perfect my hooking, my throwing-in ability and my captaincy. Derrick is such a perfectionist that I know I'll never be able to measure up to the standards he has set, but I'll keep on trying. If he hadn't taken me under his wing then I'd still probably be playing for the Trades. Quite simply, I regard Derrick as one of the most gifted coaches Hawick and Scotland have ever had and under his guidance I cannot see why Scotland should not become capable of beating anyone else in the world.

Following Derrick as coach was Ian Barnes, a big strapping forward who was, of course, a product of Hawick. On the face of it Barney, as he was known to all and sundry, was an entirely different kettle of fish from Grant. So much so that the selection committee complained at times that we weren't training hard enough. But in fact Barney had a bit of that Grant steel in him. Training was different . . . but just as hard. Everything was done in short, sharp bursts. Certainly the proof of the pudding was that Hawick continued to be successful.

However Barney, it was no secret, had a running feud with certain members of the committee and at the end of two successful years was sacked from the coaching post, never to return to Hawick. I think it was a messy chapter in Hawick's illustrious history which will not be forgotten. No explanation appeared to be given and Barney won't, I think, rest until one is forthcoming.

You can imagine it was difficult for a new coach when the players were not at all happy with the committee. I was captain at the time and it was partly my job to calm the boys down and get on with the

Alan Goodfellow: Jedforest. Goodie can'na catch me.

game. We were very lucky to get Brian Hegarty — who is still the club coach — to take over the reins. Brian and I had been in the team together as fellow forwards for a long time so we were on the same wavelength. Within a month Brian had been accepted by all the players and we were on song for another championship title.

Like the late Sam Goldwyn the cheery Hegarty can churn out the odd memorable phrase. One I liked particularly was when we were having a training session and he ordered us "to spread out in a bunch". I also recall a typical Hegarty remark when Hawick were touring in America in 1983. Our code words for throwing the ball into the line-out were based on the word Front. So if you wanted to get a ball into the front of the line-out you'd call out some word beginning with f, or r and so on. Brian was playing in this particular game and wanted a ball thrown to the front of the line-out. Philadelphia, he shouted, with a broad grin. Seriously,

35

however, I think Brian has served his apprenticeship well. He's respected by the players and in the great tradition of Hawick coaches, he puts everyone through to the limit of their endurance and a wee bit beyond.

Going outwith the Border district another coach who springs to mind is Nairn MacEwan, who went as player-coach with the Scottish squad on the Far East tour of 1977. I've never come across a more patriotic man. Even when we were abroad Nairn would ensure there was bagpipe music played in the dressing rooms before we took the field. He nicknamed me Action Man because I was here, there and everywhere, for I was desperately keen to make my mark on the tour.

Nairn was another of those coaches who liked to get their pound of flesh. At the end of every training session he'd throw down what he called the Golden Gauntlet. This consisted of doing all kinds of exercises and culminated in an all-out charge from one end of the pitch to the other . . . and all on top of a normal hard training stint.

I think Nairn was unlucky in that later he took over the national coaching job when the team was in a transitional stage. Old hands like Ian McLauchlan, Sandy Carmichael, big Al McHarg and Gordon Brown were vanishing from the scene, while the new boys like myself and John Rutherford were still learning what life was all about in the top reaches of rugby. Still, I must say I really enjoyed working under Nairn, whose only fault — if he had one at all — was that he didn't seem to know quite whether he wanted to continue playing, which he loved, or to devote himself full-time to the committee side of the game.

It was of course the legendary Jim Telfer who took over from Nairn as national coach. If Telfer figures largely in my recollections it's because he had such an influence, not only on my career but on the whole pattern of Scottish rugby.

The first time I was abroad with him was on a short ten-day tour of France in 1980 when we played three games. We were really cuffed in the first one and it was an angry Telfer that figuratively, and sometimes literally, took us by the scruff of our necks. In those days, even more than now, winning was the only thing that counted with Jim. Coming second best was death to him and I still remember that short period in my career as one of the hardest rugby stints I've ever had to overcome.

Other tours followed — to New Zealand in 1981 and the

successful visit to Australia in 1982. It wasn't until that Aussie tour that I really got to know the man and he got to know the boys. The point was that Jim, like Derrick Grant, had been such a one-minded player himself that he expected everyone else to be in the same mould. All did their damnedest to live up to his expectations but not everyone was capable of doing it his way. So it was quite a relief all round when he at last started to listen to the viewpoints of the men who were going out on the field.

When the final whistle went at Murrayfield in 1984 to mark our Grand Slam victory everyone knew that a lion's share of our success was due to Jim. He gave up the national coaching job at the top of the tree but I still feel he was a distinct loss.

His successor was Colin Telfer — no relation — who had been assistant coach but concerned almost exclusively with the backs, for he had been a fine stand-off for Hawick and Scotland. Through no fault of his own Colin didn't really have the depth of experience required for the job. Like all coaches he asked the boys to go to hell and back for him. But I think deep down — and I say this without disparagement — he realised he hadn't done all that himself.

Apart from Jim being a hard act to follow, Colin took over when the rampaging Australians were touring here and they took us apart. Then the 1984/85 season produced a whitewash for Scotland, which was perhaps understandable after the giddy heights of the Grand Slam season but was nevertheless disappointing to everyone. After that disastrous season Colin, with business pressures mounting for him, decided to call it a day and give way to Grant.

Personally I'm glad to have served alongside all these men, from each of whom I learned about my rugby craft, but Jim Telfer and Derrick Grant must be my choices as the top men in Scotland of recent years.

To revert back to my roots, I always reckon the best thing that ever happened to me was to be born in Hawick, steeped in the tradition of rugby. I was lucky, of course, that my father was Peter Deans, who died earlier this year and whom I miss greatly still. He was known to everyone in the town as a fine hooker and for many years I was known as 'Peter Deans's son' and I'm proud about that.

I've met people from all over the world and when they find out where I come from, they inevitably say, "Of course Hawick . . . famous for its knitwear and its rugby." I may be biased but I think rugby has put my home town on the world map just as much as the famous knitwear that is produced there. Practically everyone who has played for the club wants to put something back when they've decided to hang up their playing boots, whether its refereeing or doing committee work or coaching the up-and-coming boys. Most officials have been deeply involved in the game and it's great to have the backing of men who know what they are about. They'll tell you that all Hawick supporters wear green glasses and that may well be true. We're very lucky in that we have our own supporters club, many members of which never miss a game at home or away.

As most folk know, certainly in Scotland, the Border clubs have their own Border League set-up which is apart from the national championship league. And let me tell you any Border League game is no place for the faint of heart. Mind you, sometimes I'm convinced that you're better off being out on the pitch playing rather than taking your chance with the spectators. Our big game, no matter the respective strength or weakness of the clubs in any given season, is Hawick versus Gala. This is rugby's nearest equivalent to a Celtic-Rangers football match.

There is one famous story which has passed into Border rugby legend concerning Arthur 'Hovis' Brown, a great wee fellow who played for Scotland at full-back, and who turned out for Gala against us. Our scrum-half at the time was, I'm pretty sure, Harry Whittaker. In any case there was what you might term a little misunderstanding between the two players. Now Arthur's mum was a tremendous Gala supporter and also, naturally, a great fan of her son. Whatever happened, she decided it wasn't cricket, let alone rugby. As the referee didn't seem too concerned she took the law into her own hands, ran out on to the pitch and started to belabour the hapless Harry over the head with her umbrella.

Not all the spectators go as far as that of course but nearly everyone at a Border rugby ground is an expert or certainly reckons he or she is. This intense interest is good for the club and the players. You're certainly not allowed to become a big-head. I know that from the time I get into the clubhouse bar for a pint immediately after the game until I'm walking along the street on Monday, someone is bound to stop me and wonder why this or that move hadn't been properly carried out and why a pass had gone astray. It's all part of Hawick life and I reckon we have the best support in the world.

Triumphant at Mansfield.

The set-up for rugby in the town is somewhat unique. For instance, we don't have a Hawick 2nd XV. I always say we have four because of our system of feeder clubs, but if we did field a 2nd XV I'd lay money they'd give most first division sides in Scotland a fright.

Rugby begins at the primary school where Bill McLaren has done so much to encourage the boys. Progress continues at the High School where Jim Telfer is the headmaster and where there's a dedicated band of teacher-coaches, including one from Gala! If a boy is good enough the next step up is into one of the two under-18 sides which we call the semi-juniors — Wanderers or PSA. Then there are four junior sides and the prime aim of every laddie in Hawick is to join the Trades, Linden, YM or Harlequins. Once you've reached that stage you're in the shop window and the men who run the actual Hawick team are always on the look-out for talent. Only the chosen few actually get to pull on the famous green jersey and I count myself very lucky to have been one of them.

39

Hawick have a tradition of gradually blooding their young bucks. There's none of this gung-ho stuff. As the younger players come into the side they are looked after by the experienced boys. As you can imagine, playing alongside world-class men is a wonderful boost to anyone's morale and the better the men beside you then the better you'll play. I know that when I first came into the team I was more or less taken by the hand and introduced slowly but surely to the real world of rugby. Fantastic stuff for any young man and well worth sacrificing a lot of leisure hours to get fit enough to hold down your place.

It's perhaps worth noting that only the senior side actually train on the main Mansfield Park pitch. That means the coaches can concentrate on the 15 top players instead of having the place swarming with two or three different teams. All the various clubs have their own premises. The semi-junior sides, being composed of under-18 players, aren't permitted to have bars so they sometimes find it a bit of a struggle to make ends meet. But with plenty of goodwill and the loyal backing of the local supporters and the townspeople who buy raffle tickets and so on, they keep going.

I find that the way things are run in our town is the envy of most other clubs, and I'm talking not only about Scotland but also about teams who play in England, Wales and Ireland. Quite simply the set-up, to my mind, is the best in the business. Long may it continue.

Chapter 4

LONELINESS OF THE SHORT DISTANCE RUNNER

MANY people have asked me how easy it is to keep in trim for rugby at the top level. The simple answer is, it isn't.

All my rugby life I've tried not only to be fit, but super-fit. It would, I admit, be nice just to relax and have a pint with a pal or just sit at home with the feet up watching television. Even my wife Val thinks I'm mad when I go out on a cold winter's night, with the rain or snow coming down, to practise at Mansfield Park. "You've done it all," she says "Why not take it easy?"

But my view is that by not turning out I'd be letting down the other players, the Hawick club and — just as importantly — the townsfolk of Hawick. If you do miss a training session then, as sure as fate, the first auld worthy you meet the next day will say, "Where were you last night?" Of course if you don't want to train for the top level then that's up to you. One of the great joys of the game is that no one pushes you into things which you don't feel capable of achieving.

I've been lucky in that both my father and mother set me an example with their own athletic prowess. Indeed I think one of my mother's real sorrows was the day I failed to become the athletics champion at school. It was all sewn up. I'd piled up enough points in the various field events like the long jump, high jump, etc., to ensure that I only required to come in third in the main sprint on the day of the championships to take the title.

However, it was not to be. The previous evening I was out with the local Scouts troop.We were playing football and I dived on the ground to save a goal. I gashed my knee so badly that I required three stitches in it and I couldn't even hobble down to watch the sports the next day. The only consolation was that my old friend Raymond Corbett became the champ and, as we say in Scotland, it's nae loss what a freend gets. However my mum has never forgiven me to this day. As I've said, it was from her I inherited whatever speed I possess and that has enabled me to bring, I hope, something new to the art of hooking.

My own build-up to peak physical fitness may seem a bit strange to people who regard rugby training as purely a matter of going out to the pitch and trying out all the various moves. These are certainly important, as I'll stress later. However, the basis of all good rugby is that you must get your body into top trim. When I was doing my road running, or rather starting it, I and my pals would end the stint racing up a very steep hill near Hawick. Night after night we'd go as far as we could, always carefully marking the spot where we were forced to halt. Then the next night we'd try and go that wee bit further, even it it was only some inches. In that way stamina was built up through the sheer determination to go a bit beyond what seemed like the limit of endurance.

My love of running eventually led me to take part in some of the Border Games events which are held in the summer. When I first started participating it was an unusual thing for a rugby player to involve himself in such things. Nowadays, in the Borders at least, summer sprinting is seen as something which is a valuable aid to players and particularly to backs.

The man who was to become my brother-in-law, Colin Turnbull, was a first-rate sprinter. As I was by then courting Val, who was his wife's sister, it was natural that he should introduce me to some of the fellows who ran the sprint training schools. One of these men was Eddie Falconer under whom I trained in the summer on every Tuesday and Thursday. This was around my second season with Hawick and I was advised that if I wanted to get anywhere in rugby I'd have to fill out a bit. So I took up weightlifting and put on half a stone on my upper body. The whole summer I was hardly out of a track suit.

Power play in a vital match.

It wasn't until my third year at the sprint training school that I took part in my first big competition — at Selkirk. I don't mind telling you I was as nervous as a kitten. When you're out there, your feet in the blocks, waiting for the starter's gun, you realise that there aren't another 14 lads alongside you, looking after you, encouraging you and covering up any mistakes you make. Believe me, it's much more lonely than running out on to the Murrayfield turf. Anyway, I was lucky enough to get off to a flier and I was doing very well, I thought, until what seemed like a train came flashing past me and I was beaten into second place by the man who was the backmarker.

I came second again at Peebles and then came my biggest sprint triumph, at Jedburgh. I remember being in a bit of disgrace because I turned up late — I'd been waiting on Brian Hegarty. The 200 metres however was the final race of the afternoon. I managed to finish equal first in my heat and made the final. I was quite content and didn't think I had a hope of taking the first prize, especially as I'd been working and had eaten two or three meat pies for my lunch! That's hardly the ideal preparation for racing whether you're an athlete or a greyhound. However, Eddie Falconer came across to speak to me. He told me he had every confidence in me. I was a bag of nerves but he calmed me down.

The track at Jedburgh — it was on the rugby pitch — was all bends and that suited me. I got away to a good start and was doing well until I saw two of the runners ahead of me, running side by side. The position looked hopeless. Suddenly I saw a gap open up between them and, thanks to my rugby training, I was through in a flash, causing the man on my right to block the way of the backmarker. With two yards to go I knew I was going to win. My arms went up in the air. There was a great cheer from the big Hawick contingent and a huge grin from Eddie. No wonder. I heard later I was 6-1 and Eddie had put a few bob on me.

Sprinting and weight training can only help you in the rugby game. The rest is all sheer hard work on the pitch, whether playing or practising. If you cast your mind back you'll remember that in the past it was the winger who threw the ball in at the line-out. I had made a speciality of breaking away and getting at the opposition scrum-half as soon as I could. It was a bit of a grey area as far as referees were concerned but they gradually tightened up on that particular ploy which I carried on even when it was decided universally that hookers would throw in.

It used to be the case that a hooker just made use of getting the ball at the scrum. But I believe that you should, in rugby, always be near the ball and linking up with the rest of the forwards and the backs. So I have concentrated on getting as quickly as possible on to the loose ball, driving through the opposition front row as soon as the ball is hooked and in general capitalising on speed from the scrum.

It's rather like the modern day full-back. At one time a full-back was there to field the high ball, to kick to touch and, if necessary, put in the final tackle. Since the time of Ken Scotland however, the full-back is as much an attacking player as the most fleet-footed winger and to my mind it all makes for faster and more entertaining sport, both for the spectators and the players.

Similarly, hooking is not just about getting down in the middle of the scrum and striking for the ball. Nowadays throwing in is probably even more vital. When I first played semi-junior rugby

The art which I mastered — throwing in. (Courtesy: Bob Thomas)

and even in my first season with the Hawick senior side, the wingers would throw the ball into our line-out forwards. It didn't work very successfully but Derrick Grant was reluctant to change because he felt that by withdrawing the hooker to throw in it meant that one of the props had to move to the front of the line-out. This deprived him of a 'blocker', because in those days one prop stood between the front and the middle jumper and the other behind the middle jumper giving support and protection. However this changed in my second season with the club when it was obvious everyone else was going to be out of step but us.

I enjoyed my new role, especially as I had big Alan Tomes as the main line-out jumper and we struck up a great partnership. Of course I had to keep working at my throwing-in skills — Grant saw to that — but it seems more sensible to me to have just one man doing this chore instead of two wingers, who often don't see it as their job at all, taking it in turn. It was Derrick Grant who taught me to get as good a grip as possible on the ball before throwing and I often used to take a spare rugby ball home and just sit trying my grip. My mum always said I had 'piano' fingers and it certainly helps if your fingers are long, as you are so much more secure with your grasp.

I don't think, however much you try, that you completely guarantee the ball will land exactly where you want it 100 per cent of the time. There are so many considerations to take into account — the wind, the timing of the jump by the player to whom you are throwing and the odd off-day. You can, however, minimise the difficulties by really working hard. Night after night at the end of the normal training session I'd practise under the critical eye of the coach.

This is the method which I adopted and I hope it will be of some help to younger aspiring hookers. First, I'd make a mark on one of the goal posts. Then I'd retire six yards and keep throwing at that spot until I was at least getting to the target nine times out of ten. That was really aiming at the front line jumper. From there I'd raise the mark on the post and gradually work my way back from 12 to nine and finally six yards. Only when it was too dark to see any more was I let off the hook. It certainly improved my accuracy and, combined with my determination always to be fit, has enabled me to play rugby at the highest level.

I think the value of constant practice and my increasing ability to throw accurately was seen at its best in our game against Wales at the start of the 1984 season. Conditions were dry and perfect and we cleaned out the Welsh line-out. David Leslie played a stormer that day and I threw over the heads of the Welsh forwards time after time as David jumped at precisely the correct moment to launch yet another Scottish attack.

Being so used to gripping the ball, I'll tell you a secret ambition of mine. I'd love to play as a quarterback in American football and I think with all due modesty I could make a go of it.

The All Blacks for a long time had their own method in line-outs which involved throwing in overhand so that the ball spiralled towards the jumper. I studied that but could see no advantage in that method and nowadays the Blacks use the normal torpedo throw. The French, of course, have to be different. They use their scrum-half as the thrower. I think this came about because former skipper Phillipe Dintrans, although an excellent leader and hooker, wasn't so hot as a thrower-in, so Jerome Gallion took on that role. Although there was some criticism it seems a pretty good ploy and the French have carried it on when Daniel Dubroca, another hooker captain, took over with Pierre Berbizier at scrum-half. It might not work for a lot of countries but with a nippy scrum-half throwing in the big French players can suck in the opposition before releasing back to the scrum-half.

Chapter 5

THE LOTUS EATER

ON 11 OCTOBER 1975 Val and I were married at the local Wilton Church. On the same day Hawick were playing Edinburgh Wanderers and I must admit I couldn't settle down to enjoy the wedding reception until I had heard the score and found that Hawick had won. Then of course I started to worry about how well Billy Murray, who was hooking in my place, had played. Was my position in jeopardy?

I was bolstered however by the fact that I had that morning received a letter from the Scottish Rugby Union saying I'd been selected, along with two clubmates, Watt Davies and Bruce White, to join a Scottish Select XV to play Holland in Amsterdam. The match was only a fortnight away and it's a bit awkward to tell your wife of a few hours that you'll be enjoying yourself on the European Continent while she languishes at home. However I managed to pass the message on to Val and I must say she took it very well.

On the Saturday before the game Hawick played Jordanhill, then we Hawick fellows had to make a quick dash to Edinburgh to catch the flight for Holland where we played the national team the next day. It was a good game made all the more enjoyable for the Scots in that we won quite comfortably. After the match and a meal we were taken into Amsterdam and had a glimpse of the red light district. Of course as a newly married man that didn't particularly interest me. But, I can assure you, you don't see the sights of Amsterdam in Hawick High Street!

Anyway my first venture abroad convinced me that I could spend a happy year or two jetting around the world, staying at top-class hotels and playing rugby. Nowadays of course even young players take it in their stride when they're invited to go to Hong Kong, Bermuda or any other exotic part of the world. It's quite a contrast from the time when travelling all the way from the Borders to Glasgow or Newcastle was a big adventure. I think it underlines the fact that rugby is now enjoyed all over the world and in my view that's no bad thing for the game in general.

One of my most vivid memories of playing in 1975 was being selected for South of Scotland against the touring Wallabies towards the end of that year. The Australians fielded a much-feared winger in "Rhino" Ryan but we had our own particular Rhino in a well-kent Border figure, winger Mick Linton of Selkirk. He was the kind of guy who would not only run through a brick wall but build it himself to make sure it was strong enough to provide him with a really meaningful challenge.

The game was played at Netherdale and as we fielded a predominantly young team we weren't given a great deal of a chance. However the tourists were shocked when South took the lead in 34 minutes. It was then that John Rutherford hoisted a high ball which bounced off Ryan. Linton was up like a train to cross the line, with a couple of despairing tacklers trying in vain to stop him. Full-back Arthur Brown converted.

In the end, however, Aussie experience told and we were finally beaten 10-6. It was a good performance and pleased Ian 'Mighty Mouse' McLauchlan, the Scotland skipper who led the country to a 10-3 win soon afterwards at Murrayfield to make it ten victories in a row at the international ground for the Scots. That record ended, incidentally, in the next Murrayfield game, against France, when Scotland went down 13-6. The Scottish cause wasn't helped that day when English referee Ken Pattinson penalised skipper McLauchlan for lying in front of the ball while holding it steady for Andy Irvine to kick a goal. Later Pattinson, who disallowed the score, admitted that he had been wrong, which brought from 'Mouse' the wry comment, "I'm glad referees are human."

As my experience increased so did the number of higher grade games for which I was selected. It meant a lot more work, travelling to Edinburgh for squad sessions as well as actually playing. But I've never regretted that. Indeed I remember missing only one session — in 1980 — due to injury. I was so miserable that I vowed I'd never do so again no matter how I was feeling.

My usual routine on Sunday squad session days is to get up around 7.30 a.m., drive up to Murrayfield, get home around 4.30 p.m. exhausted, and flop on the couch with the kids clambering over me wanting to go to the baths or for a walk!

In March 1976 I flew off to Rheims with the B side, under Jim Telfer's coaching, which hoped to become the first at that grade from either Scotland or Wales to gain a victory on French territory. Once we got to Rheims we settled down for a meal and, of course, as is the custom in France, there was plenty of wine on the table. Well, when in Rome do as the Romans, we cracked — or in Rheims do what the French expect. But even as hands were reaching for bottles the wrath of Telfer descended. He confiscated all the booze, at the same time giving us a dressing down for even thinking of drinking wine on the eve of such an important match. Even without the wine, though, we couldn't get that elusive victory and went down 14-6.

I remember going for a walk in Rheims with one of the boys when an Alsatian dog started to chase us. At the time there was a big rabies scare and there were posters all over the place warning of the dangers. I reckon I sprinted harder to get away from that dog than ever I'd managed on an international rugby pitch.

Later in 1976 — in September — I had the great good fortune to be picked for an SRU President's XV which played Melrose as part of the Border club's centenary celebrations. Our side was studded with stars like Bruce Hay, Ian McGeechan, Mike Lampowski, Sandy Carmichael and Roger Uttley, and captained by Mike Biggar. We won the match by 26-12 after leading 14-3 at the interval.

Within a week I was off to Holland again to play for the South of Scotland. Under the banner of the Scottish Border Club our boys beat the Dutch Under-23 side 52-3, then next day a South of Scotland XV beat Impala, a Dutch national selection, by 36-6 at Hilversum.

I felt I had my foot on the first rungs of the ladder of rugby success and I had hoped to get into the Scottish XV picked to play the touring Japanese. As it was I had to settle for a seat on the replacement bench. However I now had my special Scottish XV badge and my very first Scotland track suit to mark the game which we won 34-9 at Murrayfield. None of us had rated Japan as being really a rugby-playing nation but the way the wee men ran around endeared them to the fans and I think they've come on a lot since those days.

That game was in September of 1976, and in the following February at Hughenden I got my second B cap against France. I enjoyed the game but we went down 19-16, despite being 13-6 in the lead in the first-half. Difficult so and so's these French at any level.

In between, South of Scotland beat Glasgow 43-0 at Kelso in a match which marked the coming of age of several of the Border players. It was South's first win in six similar fixtures and we were so delighted that I remember I harboured thoughts of perhaps going on the Lions tour to New Zealand, but it was not to be.

That same season I played against Ireland B in a match switched from Ayr to Murrayfield because of weather conditions but we went down 7-3. The result was no disgrace for Ireland had such players as the up-and-coming Tony Ward and Donal Spring in their ranks.

The big carrot still being dangled for Scotland's players was a tour of the Far East in September of 1977 and I was lucky enough to be picked for that. In all we played five games — three in Japan — and came back home with a record of 307 points for and only 47 against, having completed the nap hand of wins. I was one of 12 uncapped players in the squad and you can be sure I went all out to make a good impression, especially as Colin Fisher, who alternated with Duncan Madsen as the Scotland hooker at the time, was in the party. The player-coach on that particular safari was Nairn MacEwan, who was appointed national coach, or adviser to the captain as it was called then, when we got back home in October.

The weather in the Far East was the main problem because it was so humid. But we had some good fun and it turned out to be one of the most enjoyable tours ever. We made a long, tiring journey out, going by rail to London and then flying via Amsterdam to Bangkok. It was my longest ever trip and so determined was I to enjoy every second that I don't recall closing my eyes.

On our arrival we were met by our liaison man who was called, as far as we could make out, Norrie. But he certainly wasn't built like Norrie Rowan, the Scottish prop. He was a little Oriental gentleman with a big smile who wore a magnificent tee-shirt. Emblazoned on it was the slogan: F . . . Work, Go Fishing. The boys took him to their heart after that.

The first night at the hotel I reckon the temperature outside was around 90 degrees, very muggy. All the bedrooms were air-conditioned, which helped a bit, but Gerry McGuinness who was sharing with Mighty Mouse McLauchlan felt it a bit too much and asked the Mouse to open the windows. The obliging McLauchlan did so and the temperature became unbearable.

Next day we went out for a tough training session. It was midday and even the Thais had the good sense to stay in the shade and gawp at us running around like dervishes. From then on I knew that Noel Coward's famous song about mad dogs and Englishmen could also apply to Scotsmen. All the time we were there and in Hong Kong before we went over to Japan, I reckon each of us lost four or five pounds every training session. Sales of salt pills, orange juice and of course beer soared.

That night we had an official function to attend at the British Embassy and No.1 tour dress was ordered. That meant wearing a white shirt, tie, blazer and grey flannels, and we were really feeling the heat by the time we had that clobber on. Anyway, we set off on our bus to be met by an Embassy official dressed in Bermuda shorts and a thin Thai shirt!

When we were in Hong Kong the Young Generation Group were staying at our hotel and they kindly invited the boys as guests of honour to a little reception. Prop Gerry McGuinness, Jim Renwick and I were all sitting at a little table. There was a starter of sliced pineapple lying on what looked like a lettuce leaf. Gerry, who's a big lad, demolished his fruit in two seconds flat then asked Jim if the lettuce was to be eaten. "Suit yourself," said the bold Jim. So Gerry got tucked into the 'lettuce'. When Jim and myself turned to bring him into the conversation he pointed to his mouth and started moaning. We thought at first he was joking but when we saw him turning a weird colour and his tongue swelling we realised something was seriously wrong.

There was a bit of panic but an ambulance was called and Gerry was whipped off to hospital. He got out next day neither looking nor feeling very much like his old self. Being a gentleman, however, he went round to the hotel to thank the head waiter for helping the previous evening by arranging for the ambulance. The head waiter said, "I've been here five years, and I've never seen anyone attempt to eat a poisonous lotus leaf, which was what was on your plate. Why did you do it?"

"Listen, pal," said Gerry, "where I come from in Glasgow you eat everything that's put down to you."

Our first breakfast in Japan was a memorable experience. The Japs were very hospitable and when we went down we expected the usual hearty rugby meal of bacon, egg and sausage. Instead we all got plates of egg and chips. Word had got around that the only meal the British ate at breakfast was egg and chips.

Accommodation on the tour varied from the wonderful to the woeful. One night in Japan we stayed at a monastery type of building where the only thing in each room was a mattress — no tables or chairs or even a lock on the door. On top of that we had to do our washing ourselves. So big Donald Macdonald as duty boy was detailed to carry out this task. I doubt if Donald had ever washed even a hankie before. He gathered everything into one heap, our white training shorts, red tee-shirts, underpants, the lot and put them all together in one washing machine. You can imagine the result. From then on we wore pink underpants, pink shorts and pink tee-shirts.

The tee-shirts, incidentally, were a gift from a bus company who naturally had their logo on them. In those days the Scottish Rugby Union — or certain members — were so strict that a special meeting was called and we were solemnly warned that the only way we could wear the shirts was by turning them inside out.

Before we left Japan we had another example of this blinkered thinking. One of the Royal Princesses presented each player with a personally inscribed watch, a wonderful gesture to mark a highly successful tour. Again a special meeting was called and we were solemnly warned that we'd have to insult our hosts by handing back the watches because they were of more value than the limit laid down by the international board.

George Thomson, the assistant tour manager, broke this news to us. There was what you could describe as a pregnant pause. Then the uncompromising Mighty Mouse spoke up. "George," he said, "if you want this watch back you'll have to cut off my arm." I draw a veil over what happened to the watches and the temper of the players.

However I think it's fair to say that we all — administrators and players — learned a lot from that tour. For instance the only medical supplies we seemed to carry were aspirins which were used to treat everything from bruises to dysentery. I had to go to hospital when I staved my thumb during the tour and landed up waiting for **X-ray results in a room full of acupuncture patients with needles** which looked about two feet long sticking out of them. Nowadays on tours we take our own doctor and physio and it makes all the difference. There is also in general a better understanding now, in particular among the selectors, coaches and players, which helps to produce a happier atmosphere.

Talking of happiness, I was pleased personally not only with the social side but the playing part of the tour. My main rival, Colin Fisher, who didn't really do himself justice on the safari, was injured, so I played in the final match against the national Japanese team in the Olympic Stadium at Tokyo. We ran out winners by 74-9, in all scoring 11 tries.

After the match the Japanese boys wouldn't shake hands and quite honestly I thought they were in the huff. In fact we learned that they were too ashamed, thinking they had let us down by not giving us a hard enough match. I wish that attitude would spread to teams in the Parc des Princes, Cardiff's National Stadium and Twickenham!

We were walking on air as we stepped off the pitch after that particular match. Brigadier Frank Coutts, who was at the time SRU President, turned out with his bagpipes to add a bit of Scots culture to the occasion.

I had been in the wars myself, for I lost the gumshield I'd carefully worn all through the tour just before the big game. As luck would have it a little Japanese player swung his boot as I dived for the ball and I got up to spot my two front teeth sticking out. Fortunately the referee Peter Hughes, an Englishman, was a dentist and he did a quick job of sticking my teeth back again. The irrepressible McLauchlan came over to see what had happened and snapped at me, "Why didn't you wear a gumshield?" I explained I'd lost it and he took his out, jammed it in my mouth and said, "Well, wear mine." I didn't know whether to be grateful or sick.

Before leaving the Land of the Rising Sun a mock court was convened, with the huge Alan 'Toomba' Tomes as judge, to impose fines for anyone who had committed an offence during the tour. Poor Gerry McGuinness, who had nearly died from his lotus-eating exploit, was found guilty of gluttony. He was sentenced to eat a huge cream cake with his hands tied behind his back and by the time he'd done that he looked as bad as when he'd consumed the lotus leaf.

Finally, after having torn through the Far East like a hurricane, I suppose it was only right that we should leave Tokyo at the tail end of a real one.

Chapter 6

HAPPINESS IS A SCOTLAND CAP

BACK home after the heat of the exotic East to the cold of a typical Scottish winter and a bit of a disappointment for the South on 17 December 1977 at Hughenden. We had been going for a second outright district win, but Glasgow were so ably led by McLauchlan and their young Ayr full-back John Brown was in such tremendous form that it was not to be. The eventual 19-6 win by Glasgow meant a three-way split for the title between Edinburgh, South and Glasgow.

The props that day at Hughenden for the winners were McLauchlan and Sandy Carmichael, and when my next big opportunity to prove my potential came in the Murrayfield trial on 7 January 1978 they were my props in the Blues team. I was able to build up a 3-0 strike advantage early against Duncan Madsen, then in the Scotland hooking berth, although he pinched one back later. It would be nice to record a Blues win but in fact we went down by two points, 20-18, to the determined Whites. Without wishing to take anything away from the junior side, such a result is often the case, with the uncapped players going all out to prove a point and the senior fellows in their ranks — like Madsen — knowing they are fighting to retain their places.

Anyway, I managed to get a replacement berth in the Scots team

1st Cap v France, Braid Hills Hotel. Brian Hegarty, Norman Pender, Alan Tomes, Jim Renwick: A helping hand from my Hawick teammates.

to play Ireland in Dublin later that month while my old pal Brian Hegarty made the full team when injury caused David Leslie to stand down. We left Murrayfield to proceed to Edinburgh Airport where a team photo was taken. I thought it was for the full team and reserves and duly lined up. In fact it was a call for only the senior side and I shouldn't have been beaming away. However, as someone was to quip later that season, maybe I knew something that even the selectors didn't know.

When we got to Dublin I found my room-mate was Roy Laidlaw, who was another replacement. That suited me fine for Roy is a wonderful companion to have on any trip and we've been around a long time together. Roy also comes from a Border town — Jedburgh — so we both lapped up the luxury living at the Shelbourne Hotel which was then the poshest in the city.

The only trouble was the Irish team were also staying there and it put a strain on both sides if the players met on the stairs or in the lifts. Hospitality and friendship after the game is great, but you don't feel like smiling at the enemy before then. We were so close indeed that on the Friday night the Scots boys went to the cinema. It was dark when we got there, but when the lights went up at the interval there was the whole Irish squad sitting in the row in front of us. Nowadays that has all changed and the Scots boys stay well outside the city, only coming into a hotel when the match is over.

When we got to Lansdowne Road on the Saturday I wore my No.17 reserve jersey with pride and as the game went on I fancied my chances of having it changed to No.2 in the not too distant future. This was the match where Doug Morgan, the scrum-half captain, made a decision which is still argued about. In the dying minutes Scotland were trailing 12-9 when a simple-looking penalty chance presented itself. Instead of going for what looked a certain one point away from home — always a big factor at the start of an international season — Doug elected to run the ball. The 50,000 strong crowd applauded — so would I had I been Irish. We didn't get the try and came home without a thing, except a little suffering from Irish post-match hospitality.

I said then, and I stick to it now, that Morgan was wrong. In fairness, Doug himself said, "The enjoyment in rugby is winning. This was our big chance to snatch victory and remain live contenders for the Triple Crown." He's still wrong in my book.

I returned to Hawick with a sneaky impression that I had a good chance of being selected for the next game which was against France. As soon as I was back on the Sunday I was out doing my usual road training, but running through my mind all the time was the thought of whether or not I would be picked.

On the Tuesday night, when the Scottish selectors met in Edinburgh, I went down to the club to train. At the time I lived only a few doors from Robin Charters, who was a selector, and I thought he might drop in to tell me if I was in the team. But 11 p.m. came and went without any word and I went to bed to try and sleep.

The postman didn't come round our way until about 9.30 a.m. and I had to take Val to her work and start myself long before that. But I couldn't settle. I had to ask away and raced to the house. There was the same kind of letter which had told me I was to be a replacement for Ireland but this time it contained the magic words,

1st Cap 1978: whose a pretty boy then?

"You have been selected for Scotland."

Although I had trained and prayed for this moment for years I was still stunned. I sat on the stairs reading the words again. And of course I soon found something else to worry me, for it said I would collect a WHITE jersey with the No.2 on it (to avoid

59

clashing with the light blue of the French). I now wondered desperately if I could hang on to my place and pick up the traditional BLUE jersey of Scotland. Fortunately for the sake of Val's peace of mind as well as my own I've succeeded in doing that.

Once I had convinced myself that the news was really true I dashed down to see Val at her work, then I visited my father and mother with the news. My dad was pretty quiet, merely offering me his congratulations, but I knew he was feeling proud.

The first 'outsider' to whom I broke the news was Raymond Telfer's wife Marion. Raymond was on the Hawick committee and his wife was Greens-daft and served the teas every week. When she saw me she said, "Are you in?" When I replied "Yes" she said, "Good, you deserve it." That made me feel really chuffed. I was a bit late getting back to work but no one minded . . . it's not every day you get a new cap in your town and in a place like Hawick everyone shares in the joy.

Usually a new cap doesn't play on the Saturday before an international. After all, it would be a real blow after years of preparation to be hurt in a club game. However, I felt I needed some practical rugby after missing some games and sitting on the bench in Ireland. So I played for Hawick against Roundhay, suffered no harm, and we got a victory to boot. That night Val and I celebrated with a hoarded bottle of champagne . . . and fish and chips.

The next day or two were really long. I was scared I might catch flu but I survived until the Thursday when the Hawick contingent climbed into Norman Pender's car and eventually arrived at Edinburgh, shaken by his driving but otherwise raring to go. We had a tough training session then retired to our team headquarters at the Braids Hotel, where Scottish teams have gone for around the last 20 years. It's one of those places with its own atmosphere and the boys regard it as a home from home.

There's a certain tradition to the build-up for an international match and now that I was a member of the senior team I took an even greater interest in it than when I was merely a replacement.

After the training session we were bussed from Murrayfield to the Braids and sat down to dinner. The menu prices were away out of my range, but as the SRU were picking up the tab I soon adjusted. I still always have the same kind of evening meal before a game that I chose that night. It's prawn cocktail, scampi and fillet

*There were six Hawick players in Scotland v. Wales 1981. L-R Back: A. Cranston,
N. Pender, B. Hegarty. L-R Front: J. Renwick, A. Tomes, C. Deans.*

steak. And here's a tip for you. Always eat onions with the steak . . .
one of my old sprinting buddies assured me that runners always eat
plenty of onions because they burn up indigestive food.

We then watched videos of a couple of games, particularly one in
which Roger Quittenton had been in charge. It's always handy to
know on which areas of a game a ref is likely to concentrate. Then it
was early to bed. I was sharing with Pender who wanted to sit up

playing bridge. BRIDGE? They never taught you that at Hawick High School. Pontoon maybe, bridge never. So I was a bit of a dead loss to the big prop.

On Friday morning we were out at Murrayfield again but this time mainly for the benefit of the media who came along to get their pictures and interviews. As we were playing France of course everyone was already writing us off as having no chance which is the way we like it. In the afternoon most of us went down to a local club where we played pool or skittles, anything to take our minds off the task to come.

On Saturday morning I must have packed and unpacked my kit at least three times. It seemed ages until the bus came with its police escort. But once we got to the back of Murrayfield stand we could hear the skirl of the pipes and the adrenalin began to flow. There was the usual gauntlet of well-wishers to get by, wee laddies and grown men shouting good luck and, as he always is, my old P.E. teacher Bill McLaren standing near the team entrance.

In the dressing room I found a pile of good luck cards and telegrams — from Val, my parents, old friends — and one I appreciated particularly from Hawick Royal Albert, the town's soccer club. Eventually we got changed and I remember looking pretty dazed in the mirror with my new No.2 jersey on. McLauchlan, leading the pack, soon cut me down to size. "Come on," he said, "you'll have plenty of time to admire that after the game."

We went out to have a look at the pitch. I remember the weather was cold and damp — not really suited to the usual French type of play, was my cheering thought. Already there were about 4,000 spectators at the ground who fired off their salutations as we tested the playing surface.

Back in the dressing rooms the SRU President Lex Govan looked in to wish us well. That super-Scot Nairn MacEwan put on a Corries tape and McLauchlan, as usual, got down to business. While the skipper, Doug Morgan, gave a final briefing to the backs, McLauchlan took the forwards into the nearest bit of privacy, the toilets. One thing that sticks out in my mind is when McLauchlan pointed to the soles of his boots and said, "These aren't just for getting a grip on the pitch. They're for getting Frenchmen out of the way." It was a clear indication that he was expecting the pack to ruck any of the French who were on the ground, a technique perfected by the All Blacks and which the Scots have adopted in recent years.

At last we got into the tunnel. My mind seemed to go blank. It was 4 February 1978 but the thoughts I had were nothing to do with time and dates, but purely with emotion. It's difficult to put into words, but I said to myself I'm here playing for my family, my friends, Hawick, the South and Scotland. And just then we emerged on to the pitch and there was a crescendo of sound from what seemed to be the whole of Scotland. What an experience and how worthwhile all the time spent on getting here had been.

We had a dream start to the game, and we played like men inspired. At one time we were leading 13-0, but injuries to full-back Andy Irvine and winger Dave Shedden cost us dear.

I was the only new cap in the Scots side that day and a couple of incidents stick out in my mind. At an early scrum I got the ball and then the French prop Cholley's head in my face. As Cholley was an amateur heavyweight boxing champion you can understand why I was, to put it mildly, a bit woozy for a while. Then I got a strike against the head and I was so elated that I gave a whoop of joy. The next thing I knew was that I was on the receiving end of a fair old punch on the chin.

I learned a lesson from that. A painful one, but one which I remember to this day and abide by. If you do get a strike against the head, just keep your mouth shut. Rejoice in your heart but not your speech.

With France, who were Grand Slam champions, getting back into the game in the second period we eventually went down 19-16. Our try scorers, before they were hurt, were Irvine and Shedden. That perhaps indicates how cruel fate was to us that day. Morgan kicked a drop goal, a penalty and a conversion. France got tries through Gallion and Haget, while Aguirre, their full-back, kicked three penalty goals and a conversion.

It seemed a long, long trudge back to the dressing room we'd left only 80 minutes before with such high hopes. I felt so weary I just sat down and I may have had a wee cry I was so disappointed. But at least the boys had given it their best shot and it just hadn't come off. Hawick could take consolation in the fact that in all seven players from the club, including the two replacements who came on, had been in the match.

Everyone was very kind to us. I still have a special committee

programme which was given to me by the SRU President Lex
Govan, while coach MacEwan cheered us up by telling the media,
"This is a tremendous squad who want to play good rugby."

Once we had showered and got on the bus for the official
reception at the North British Hotel in Edinburgh we were feeling
better — even more so when John Roxburgh, who is now the
technical administrator, produced some miniatures of Drambuie
while we were on our way. A lot of the more seasoned boys opened
their bottles after the usual autograph signings for the ball boys.
But I kept mine intact, not only because I had yet to acquire a taste
for the stuff, but because I wanted to keep it as a souvenir in case I
didn't get picked again.

We had been a bit down when we left but we all knew we had
played well and we soon began to perk up. Once we got back to the
North British Hotel it was a case of finding out where we were
staying for the night and then McLauchlan came up to my room to
tell me we were all to gather across the road at the Cafe Royal as
soon as possible for a pint.

Well, the place was packed with French supporters, one of whom
had a bugle. Somehow or other Jim Renwick, who used to be in the
Salvation Army and was really a good musician, got mixed up with
this particular supporter. The Frenchman played, then Jim took
over and gave us a rendering of *Tally-ho* which had everyone in the
place cheering, especially the French. We were clapped and
cheered out of the place to go back across the road for the
President's traditional reception. I was wearing a dinner suit for
the first time — it cost me around £40 then and it turned out to be a
bargain with the number of dinners I've since attended.

We had a couple of drinks with the President who at the time was
Lex Govan and then went down to mingle with the guests. They
included a cross section of everyone in rugby from clubs all over the
country, coaches of mini and midi rugby, ex-Presidents of the SRU
and some managing directors of business companies. Most of them
came up to sympathise with us on our losing and to wish us better
luck the next time.

Then it was into the official dinner — my first — where I had
Norman Pender, almost a father figure to me, sitting beside me.
There's always a cigar beside your plate as part of the dinner and,
of course, there's white and red wine. The Scots boys sat at one
table, the French at another. We had a good meal then the Scots

boys started a sing-song. The French I found to be very sedate whereas we thoroughly enjoyed ourselves.

Speeches began around 9.15 p.m. with the two Presidents of Scotland and France and both captains speaking for about five minutes each. Then we players were free to go and meet our wives or girlfriends. They had been having a meal which they had to pay for themselves while the committee wives had their own special meal in those days, with the SRU paying for them. Anyway, I saw Val in one of the bars in the hotel and we chatted and had a drink with one or two supporters. Then off to the dance in the same hotel.

It's probably the most exclusive dance in Scotland for there's no way you can get in without a ticket and the doorman, a very nice guy, has a sixth sense about keeping out any intruders. Well, we danced the night away and with the strains of *Auld Lang Syne* ringing in our ears eventually got off to bed in the wee sma' hours. Up again in the morning to face a cooked breakfast which, strangely enough, I enjoyed and still do after a game then back to Hawick late on Sunday morning.

That's the traditional kind of pattern for after-match festivities in Edinburgh. In Paris the setting is perhaps more resplendent — not perhaps, it certainly is — at the Grand Hotel.

The dinner itself is held in a most magnificent, mirrored room and it's certainly not the kind of place you can imagine a rowdy rugby dinner taking place without some damage. But whether we're always over-awed by the sheer luxury of the place, I've never seen any damage done. The Germans used the Grand during the war when they occupied Paris and it must be said their taste in that particular matter was pretty good.

My first dinner there coincided with the fact that Scotland, although beaten, had played very well and also Roddy had been born on the Tuesday before the match. In those days we used to stay at the Normandie — now we go to a place well outside the city centre — and once we had left the ground and had the President's reception I went across with the boys to the nearest café and produced a box of 50 half Coronas which I had bought, duty free of course, on the way over so we could celebrate Roddy's birth in style.

The French beer hardly appealed to a Scot so it was wine or spirits and Pernod became the favourite tipple. Once back at the Grand we switched to Buck's Fizz — a mixture of champagne and orange juice — and began a game of forfeits. This meant the more answers you got wrong the more 'Fizz' you had to drink. Then we went into dinner to be served a lethal mixture of white wine, red wine, champagne, etc . . . Spirits were getting a bit high by this time and we loosed off a few rolls at the Press boys. Robin Charters soon put a stop to that and when we tried to get a sing-song going it was halted. Meantime the French were very reserved. A TV crew were in the room doing interviews at their table and the players refused to join in with us. Maybe they thought we were too rowdy.

I remember that night ending with all the boys wearing their napkins round their foreheads — à la Rambo — and Roger Baird and myself getting marooned at our table and being pelted with everything from cream to sugar. It was a hell of a night but no damage was done and the high jinks were due to this mixture of wines and spirits. Normally we would be having a couple of pints. There was also the influence of the 'Benghazis'. This meant anyone could suddenly call 'Benghazi!' and you all had to stand up and drink whatever happened to be in your glass.

My old friend Iain 'The Bear' Milne is a guy who loves these Paris trips. But the people he hires his dinner suit from in Edinburgh aren't quite so enthusiastic. For Iain goes through these suits like a spendthrift through a fortune. You can bet your life that when the suit, usually I suspect the oldest one in the shop, is returned either the jacket is ripped or the trousers are damaged or both. On one memorable occasion The Bear tried to vault a dustbin, came down heavily and both knees were out of his trousers. But he always enjoys himself and there's no harm in him, as witness the fact that one of our gendarme escorts gladly gave the big fellow a lift back to the team hotel on the back of his motor bike!

Another prop and friend of mine, Gerry McGuinness, has less happy memories of Paris. On his first visit he got slightly carried away with it all. He, I and Norrie Rowan were at a night club with some of the French players when Gerry felt ill. I always remember that there was a lovely marble staircase which an old lady was just finishing cleaning. Gerry tried to make the toilet but couldn't and was ill. I think I'd rather have faced Cholley than the cleaning woman as she bounded up the stairs waving her mop and we made a rapid exit.

But of course the real purpose in visiting Paris is not to have high jinks but to play rugby against what is always a formidable team.

One of the great scrum-halves to grace rugby, Jerome Gallion. I won the race this time. (Courtesy: James Galloway)

Of all the French players I've come up against the former skipper Jean-Pierre Rives must surely be the most outstanding. He's not very tall but he's strong and fast. I've often wondered how he survived some games. I've seen him in Australia with a damaged shoulder, blood streaming from his head and still rallying his troops. A great man. He and Jean-Claude Skrela, the other wing-forward, complemented each other beautifully.

The first front row of the French I played against was Paparemborde, Paco and Cholley. That trio could hold their own against the much-vaunted Pontypridd front row any time. Paparemborde is a very strong prop, Paco a chunky hooker and of course Cholley is a boxer who, believe it or not, is a very nice guy off the field but really hard when he's playing.

Other distinguished French players I recall are the ex-skipper Bastiat, a huge No.8, Orso who has a farm near Nice and has invited Val and myself over for a holiday, and of course Jacques Fouroux, now the distinguished French coach. Known as the Little General in his playing days Fouroux was a fantastic scrum-half. His pass with a flick of the wrist from the base of the scrum or the line-out was something to marvel at even if he was fortunate enough to play behind a tremendously good pack.

Then came another great scrum-half in Jerome Gallion, who played against Scotland in the 1984 Grand Slam match at Murrayfield. I've always felt that the turning point in that match was when Gallion had to go off after a collision with David Leslie. He was the man who for my money made the French side tick.

The full-back Serge Blanco is an enigma. He's world-class on his day. He's so fast and so exciting to watch. But if you can hoist a few high balls and he spills them then you're in with a shout. He's either great or rubbish . . . no half measures. And I could not talk about great French players without a mention of Phillipe Sella. He is to my mind one of the best centres — if not the best — we've seen in world rugby for the past ten years. His handling is superb, his running exciting and very, very swift. He's a very aggressive centre despite the fact that he's of slight build. A must to be included in any team of the decade.

On the Wednesday following my international debut against France the letter arrived which I'd been waiting so hopefully for, informing me that I'd been picked to play against Wales at Cardiff Arms Park (now the National Stadium) on 18 February.

I thought the Sunday squad session after that went pretty well but big Al McHarg wasn't happy about my throwing-in, which upset me a bit. However by Thursday of the following week at the final training session we were on song. One thing which McLauchlan kept harping on about was the much-vaunted front row who were turning out for Wales. Up until then I'd never given them a thought, but by the time Ian had finished warning us of the danger there I felt they must be in the super league.

Poor Andy Irvine hadn't recovered from the injury to his left shoulder although the SRU selectors gave him until the last possible minute, so he was ruled out of the party, and Bruce Hay was selected at full-back, with Bill Gammell on the right wing.

Once in Cardiff the Scots settled in at the Park Hotel, which is in the city centre and only five minutes bus ride away from the ground. On Saturday morning after breakfast in the hotel I bumped into some of the Jed-forest boys who were chatting with Roy Laidlaw. We all had a good crack, which kept my mind off the match.

Seen any goldfish? (Courtesy: Bob Thomas)

YOU'RE A HOOKER, THEN

When we had a look at the pitch it was in good nick but the snow which had been cleared off it was piled high round the perimeter. While I tried not to think too much about the opposition there's no doubt that the Welsh team we played was one of the great sides. It was a great game but we ended up losing by 22-14.

I don't mind admitting losing five strikes against the head because the formidable Welsh pack, which included Charlie Faulkener, Bobby Windsor and Graham Price up front with Jeff Squire, Derek Quinnell and Terry Cobner in the back row, kept pressurising our scrum. In addition it was the Scottish scrum-half, in this case Morgan, who called out the verbal signal when he was going to put the ball in. After that match I changed to a hand signal which at least lets the scrum-half know when the hooker is ready to strike.

The Welsh backs were at least as good as their forwards, with Gareth Edwards picking up his 51st cap and Phil Bennett playing behind him at stand-off. Gerald Davies, Steve Fenwick and the great full-back J.P.R. Williams were all on duty.

I thought our boys did well to get 14 points and I was delighted to see big Alan Tomes, my Hawick clubmate, scoring a try from a perfectly executed penalty move. Another Hawick man, Renwick, got the Scots other try while Morgan kicked two penalty goals. However Wales scored four tries to our two and skipper Bennett added a drop goal and a penalty. There was no doubt the home team deserved their win.

After the match we were entertained very hospitably by the Welsh, who were in fine singing form, as their supporters had been earlier. I don't know what it is about Welsh fans but once you hear them sing, even if their team is trailing, you know Wales are going to win in the end.

Snow had been falling just when the final whistle went and when we left the Angel Hotel where the official reception was held there was about a foot of it lying. Treacherous stuff it was too and Brian Hegarty slipped and cracked his head. He was unconscious for a couple of minutes before we managed to get him to his feet and our team headquarters.

Next morning practically every road out of Cardiff was cut off by the snow, including the one to the airport where our plane was waiting. So it was decided to try and reach Birmingham by bus and pick up a flight there. It was a terrible journey which took three or four hours and it was dark by the time we got to the airport. However our plane was waiting and everyone climbed aboard with feelings of relief. Off we taxied and just as we were ready to rise suddenly the lights went out, the brakes went on and it got really scary, particularly when we looked out of the windows and saw the airport fire engines screeching alongside. After taxi-ing around the airport we were asked to leave the plane, which we were quite glad to do by that stage. Eventually we were able to get back to the departure lounge. Some of the boys had their wives with them on the trip and I think that experience would probably discourage most of the women from demanding to travel with hubby again, although in all fairness — and touching wood — that's the only air hitch I've had in my time playing for Scotland.

We were darned lucky to get away at all. Traditionally a lot of Scots clubs — expecially from the Borders — go down to Wales every second year at the time of the international to play some village team and when the Welshmen come to Scotland they reciprocate. However the conditions were so bad that several of the teams — indeed I think our national side was the only one which got away — were stranded for up to three days. It may not have gone well with the missus but the boys left made the most of it and when they ran out of money the Welsh just had a whip-round to see they weren't short of a pint. That's rugby for you.

Next we had to prepare for the final game of the season, against England at Murrayfield on 4 March. It was obvious there would be at least one change, for our injury jinx had struck again and big McHarg had broken two bones in his left hand against Wales. Then Dave Shedden, that incredibly courageous winger, had to go into hospital for a cartilage operation after damaging his knee, again in the Welsh match. The final blow was when Ian McGeechan broke down on the Friday before the game with an ankle injury which appeared to have cleared up. All in all, it didn't augur well for our chances against a strong England team, especially as the game between our countries is always a do-or-die effort.

Chapter 7

HOW PRINCE PHILIP DODGED A HAY-MAKER

MY FEARS about the outcome of the 1978 Calcutta Cup match proved only too well-founded. We had two new caps, with the huge lock David Gray coming in for McHarg and Richard Breakey replacing McGeechan at stand-off. Although this was to be Breakey's only cap I regarded him as a very good player. He was a regular and popular member of the Scottish squad for a long time, travelling for training sessions from the North of England where he played for Gosforth.

The eventual score of 15-0 was a pretty fair indication of how badly we had been beaten. It was the first England victory at Murrayfield since 1968 and I don't mind admitting I was relieved when the Irish referee John West blew the final whistle. I had lost six or seven strikes during the game, something which every hooker hates. But there was no doubt that the English pack had much more strength than we did and we were pushed off the ball time after time. Their forward line-up that day was: Barry Nelmes, Peter Wheeler, Fran Cotton, Billy Beaumont (captain), Maurice Colclough, Peter Dixon, John Scott and Mike Rafter.

So Scotland ended the season with the wooden spoon and overall it had been a sad introduction to rugby at international level for me personally. However, I had been more than grateful to hold on to my position and to have the opportunity of learning so much more about the game which has virtually been my life for the past nine or ten years.

In particular I had great support and encouragement from Ian McLauchlan, whom I rate as one of the best prop forwards ever to wear a Scottish jersey. It was McLauchlan who drilled into me the subtleties of hooking the ball to help your backs as much as possible. For instance, you'll notice that in Scotland, because we have a light pack, we tend to use channel one perhaps more than others. This means that I, as hooker, try and keep my feet together as much as possible. When the scrum-half puts the ball into the scrum I then swing the ball through the loose-head (No.1) prop's legs as quickly as possible. This means that when properly done it misses out the second row man and reaches the scrum-half, who has taken up his post again, in a flash. He in turn whips the ball out to the stand-off and in John Rutherford we're lucky to have a player who can beat any opposition provided he receives quick possession.

Of course you can't carry out this ploy every time and if you are under severe pressure in the front row the McLauchlan tip is to use channel two. This calls for the hooker to extend his left leg as far to the left as possible and swing the right leg, bringing the ball under your body then striking it between the centre of the two second row men to make it land at the feet and hands of your No.8.

Channel three ball is rarely tried because we like to get the ball away fast but in brief it means striking the ball so that it virtually comes out in front of the right hand wing forward.

Another tip I'm grateful to Ian for was his advice to take up weightlifting. He himself was a bit of a keep-fit fanatic and he was immensely strong. I took his tip and it benefited me greatly for I put on a badly needed half stone on my upper body at a time when some people were saying I was too light for international rugby.

But the main thing McLauchlan did for me was to give me encouragement. I think a lot of young players would have felt like giving up after the results of my first season in international rugby. However, 'Mighty Mouse' kept me going and he was always willing to help and to pass on some of his own vast store of experience. At that stage in a player's career when you're really just starting you shut up and try and absorb everything you can from the older boys.

It was a sad day for me and, I feel, Scottish rugby when Ian went. The one consolation is that our present loose-head prop, David Sole, looks like being another McLauchlan.

As I have mentioned earlier, I also at this time worked on a tap system of signals to let my scrum-half know when I was ready to strike for the ball. This is much more satisfactory to a hooker than listening for a call from the scrum-half that the ball is coming in. Apart from anything else, in most internationals the cheering and shouting of the crowd means you can hardly hear yourself think, let alone strain your ears to hear your colleague. The only snag I've found is that should an opposing prop grab your arm or hand, preventing you doing your tap signal, then you're in trouble. In general, however, it works well.

I know earlier this season when we were playing Ireland at Murrayfield we were scrummaging so low that I couldn't even see my feet, let alone my scrum-half. But Roy Laidlaw, who was on duty that day, and I have played , I reckon, about 100 games together at various levels so now we have what you could describe as a telepathic understanding.

Anyway, at the end of the wooden spoon season Hawick were invited to take part in the prestigious Middlesex Sevens at Twickenham. Alas we were well and truly dumped out in the second round and in view of the great reputation Border clubs have for playing the abbreviated game, we felt we had let down Scottish rugby somewhat.

However you can't, in life or sport, afford to give up and the chance of playing against the magical All Blacks in December proved a powerful incentive for every player with ambition to get fit and keep fit. When the great day dawned on 9 December 1978 at Murrayfield the Blacks, under a wonderful skipper in flanker Graham Mourie, were going for their first ever Grand Slam over the home countries. What a team they put out: Brian McKechnie; Stuart Wilson, Bruce Robertson, Bill Osborne, Bryan Williams; Doug Bruce, Mark Donaldson; Brad Johnstone, Andy Dalton, Gary Knight, Andy Haden, Frank Oliver, Lester Rutledge, Gary Seear and Mourie.

It was one of those dreich Scottish days, the rain soaking the fans and the Lion Rampant flags carried by many of the faithful 70,000. The skies were so overcast that the kick-off time was brought forward five minutes and even then the match ended in gloom. With their traditional black jerseys the New Zealanders always

The Lion's Roar — or is it a Lion bored?

look menacing. But that particular day they looked positively awe-inspiring. We Scots watched as they did their world-famous Haka routine and I thought, "My God, how do you play supermen like that?"

Well, we did.

Sure, Scotland finally lost 18-9 and the All Blacks achieved their Grand Slam dream. But the boys had played with so much guts that afterwards Mourie said, "They played with a spirit of adventure we hadn't encountered in our previous internationals. Scotland should be proud of their team."

I was, let me say, particularly pleased with two aspects of the game. One was that my old friend Bruce Hay, playing on the wing, had the honour of being the first Scot to score a try against the All Blacks since 1935. Mind you, I've since kidded him that he scored over his best distance — two yards! Our other points that day came from a drop goal by Ian McGeechan, who was skipper, and an Andy Irvine conversion.

The other important bonus for me about that particular match was getting to know my opposite hooker, Andy Dalton. I looked to him as world-class and since that day he and I have been great friends who still keep in touch.

However I hadn't expected to see the All Blacks again as soon as I did after the international. What happened was that Geoffrey Windsor-Lewis, the Barbarians secretary, rang a Hawick namesake of mine, Derek Deans, who had also been a Scotland hooker, and asked him down as stand-by for the Blacks' last match of their tour, against Barbarians at Cardiff. Derek was good enough to say, "I think you've got the wrong Deans", and put him in touch with me.

It was a late call and I had to hire a car for the journey. I remember it was very foggy and it was no joke driving through the night from Scotland. I got to the team hotel about 2 a.m. and was put in a wee room which I'm sure had all the heating pipes for the hotel centred on it, so I slept — or tried to — with the windows open.

Later that morning Jim Renwick, who was in the Baa-baas side, introduced me to the boys before we went along to the ground and I took my seat on the bench. I'd rather have been playing but I was glad enough just to be there, to see the All Blacks win 18-16.

Being chosen for the Barbarians, even as a replacement, is a great honour and to my mind probably the best thing a player can

hope for next to being capped for his country. The Barbarians —
no one knows exactly why they are called that — believe in open,
attacking rugby. They play all the major touring sides and selection
to their ranks is by invitation only.

The Barbarians club is unique in that it has no pitch or
clubhouse, no entry fee or subscription and no funds of its own. The
expenses of this touring team are paid by the clubs they visit. The
club started in 1890 under Percy Carpmael, a great all-round
sportsman. He was the first President and at the moment Herbert
Waddell is the fifth.

After the match Geoffrey said we could keep our jerseys, which
was unheard of. But Herbert Waddell, one of the grand old men of
Scottish rugby and the Barbarians, put a stop to that. Despite that
I still think he's a great man and of course he's respected in rugby
circles all over the world.

I did get a game for the Baa-baas shortly afterwards, against
Leicester at Leicester. This was my reward for having come down
at short notice to sit on the bench for the All Blacks match at
Cardiff. To get to Leicester I had to make a car journey on Boxing
Day from Hawick, but I was delighted to be selected in my first
international season. Once there, I found I was playing against
Peter Wheeler who was beginning to make a name for himself and
who was later to become England's captain. Leicester were at that
stage really building up to their peak and of course the match was
taken very seriously. Straw had been put down on the pitch to
make sure the game went on and when it was lifted the turf was
perfect and the lights were switched on for the 3 p.m. kick-off.

Before the match started I was in the clubhouse with Bruce Hay
who was also in the team that day when an elderly chap came up to
me and boomed out, "Hope your lads are ready to go today,
Elgan." I didn't know what he meant. But Bruce explained that
this was the great Herbert Waddell, the Barbarians President, and
he was obviously mixing me up with Elgan Rees, the Welsh winger.
Brucie thought this a great joke and to this day I'm still sometimes
called Elgan by the Scots boys who have heard the tale. I wasn't all
that chuffed but I'm glad to say that Herbie knows me pretty well
nowadays and we have struck up a great friendship.

After the very exciting match, which Leicester won, I had to
make a nightmare journey home. There was a lot of water on the
road and I didn't get in until around 1 a.m. to start work a few

hours later. But it had been well worth the effort and later in season 1985/86 I had the honour of captaining Barbarian teams which won against Italy, London Welsh and East Midlands.

Back to international business and Scotland's next big game was against Wales at Murrayfield on 20 Janurary 1979. Helped by the wind and an in-form Andy Irvine, we were nicely ahead at the interval but eventually went down 19-13. It was Scotland's eighth defeat in a row and the fans and media were getting restless. One notable point about that particular match was the first appearance in a Scottish jersey of John Rutherford, destined to be rated one of the world's best stand-off exponents.

Our next game against England at Twickenham at least broke the sequence of losses, for we drew 7-7. Mind you, I thought some of us would land in the Tower of London before the match began.

The Duke of Edinburgh was the principal guest of the English Rugby Union and of course was brought out on to the pitch to meet the teams. Now, my friend Bruce Hay has, if I may put it so, rather an up-turned nose, earned in many a tough game over the years. When the Duke reached the bold Brucie he inquired, "And which lamp post did you bump into?" Like Queen Victoria, Brucie was **NOT amused. I think the Duke was pretty lucky not to find himself** flat on his back. But fortunately he moved on quickly to the stand.

There were a few incidents in the game which stick out. There was a scare when our No.8 Ian Lambie went down with a neck injury. For a short time he couldn't move or feel anything in his arms and legs, but fortunately he quickly recovered. Then my old Gala pal Gordon Dickson put in one of the best tackles I can recollect, on Roger Uttley, the England captain. Uttley himself, I'm sure, felt bewildered as he collapsed with the force, although it was a perfectly fair tackle. There was a dramatic ending when I managed a strike against the head and John Rutherford went for the drop goal. They're always difficult to pop over and John just missed . . . otherwise he would have been awarded the freedom of Scotland.

There was one other aspect during and following this particular game which had the players scratching their heads over the logic — or rather lack of it — being shown by the SRU at the time. At Twickenham, with millions watching the teams on the TV, we were all smartly dressed in new Adidas suits. A week or so later, Gala were to be on a televised game and naturally were also going

Whose gonna wash my shorts?

to wear the same brand of jersey. But when the club sought permission they were refused and the jerseys were taken away and replaced by something else which had no advertising logos. I'm still trying to work that one out after all these years.

Whatever the dress, however, you've got to get on with the game and Scotland's next encounter, at Murrayfield against Ireland, resulted in yet another draw by 11-11. Draws are very much the exception rather than the rule in rugby and to have two on the trot is pretty well unheard of. Despite not winning, it at least gave Scotland another point and, more important, marked the introduction to international rugby of Iain Milne, the prop. Since those days Iain has become mighty well-known as 'The Bear'. I regard him as my right arm, a man who has taken on the best in the world and come out on top.

My preparations for the final game of that season — against France in Paris — were interrupted for the best possible reason, for Val was due to have our son Roddy. The baby was actually due on the weekend of the French match, but the doctors must have been rugby fans for they decided to have her into the Simpson Maternity Unit in Edinburgh to induce the birth a week before.

At first it looked plain sailing. But the child, like its father, was stubborn and poor Val was in labour for 16 hours before our son was finally delivered by operation. About 3 a.m. on the Tuesday morning I got to Hawick to tell all the parents and friends, then went back to Edinburgh. Val and the baby were both fine by now and I was fidgeting as the clock ticked on because Tuesday night is training night. It was Val who eventually said, "For goodness sake get away to Hawick and train."

I arrived at Mansfield Park after a quick visit home to pick up my kit. Just as I got there I bumped into Derrick Grant, who was the coach at the time. "Where the hell have you been?" he said. "You're late." I thought that perhaps he hadn't heard of Roddy's birth for I was expecting the usual congratulations. When I explained the circumstances, Derrick gave me a lecture about the need to plan any family so that the children are born in the summer instead of interfering with the rugby season.

Talk about dedication to the game!

Anyway, with my family now doing well I got away with the rest of the boys to Paris. One of the most frightening things about rugby there, apart from the team, is being driven to the ground with a police escort. Motor-cyclists lead the team bus, lights flashing, sirens wailing and horns hooting non-stop in a mad race through the centre of the city. Any tardy car driver who looks remotely like holding up the bus has his bodywork unceremoniously kicked. It certainly makes you so anxious about getting there in one piece that the match itself seems pretty sedate.

It was my introduction to the Parc des Princes. What an atmosphere is generated there with bands, firecrackers and fans kicking up a non-stop din from start to finish. The architecture reminds me of a Roman amphitheatre and when I glanced up at the towering stand I wouldn't have been surprised to see a Roman Emperor waiting to give the thumbs down to us poor Scottish players.

We were beaten 21-17, with the French getting the breaks in the closing stages. At least however the boys got three tries, which is a feat in itself against France in their home territory, and played really well. Indeed skipper McGeechan said afterwards, "I felt we played together better as a unit than at any other time this season." But he, and the rest of the team, dearly wanted to move from being gallant losers to victorious winners. That ambition would now have to be put off until next season.

Meantime I was picked again for the Baa-baas and went on the Easter tour where I got a game at Cardiff against the local city club. Until then I thought around 5,000 was excellent for any club match, but Cardiff drew 20,000 or 25,000 spectators to games like this. Bill Beaumont was our captain when I played that day and I had the satisfaction of scoring a try. But we had to give best to Cardiff. Terry Holmes, with that aggressive running of his, scored three tries.

I had to cut my tour short however when, after phoning home, I found Val in a bit of a state because a water pipe in our home had burst during a particularly cold spell. So I made my excuses and left.

The season ended for me with appearances in three Border Sevens tournaments in the course of which I notched up a dozen tries. This put a brighter face on things after the national disappointments.

Chapter 8

FOR WHOM THE CLOCK CHIMES

I HAD MY sights set high for a possible place in the Lions squad which was to tour South Africa in 1980 at the end of our season, but I knew there was a lot of hard work to be done if I was to be considered. First of all the All Blacks were coming over for a tour of England and Scotland. In October 1979 they played the South of Scotland at Mansfield Park.

We all met up on the Friday night in Hawick and for some reason the South selectors decided that even the local Hawick contingent should stay in a hotel in the centre of the town. I think it would have been more sensible to let us stay in our own homes and go down with the squad in the morning. It seemed strange staying in a hotel when your house was only a short distance away. What made it much worse, though, was that the hotel was near the Town Hall and the clock on the hall chimed every quarter of an hour. I got very little sleep.

However the boys were pretty confident of beating the All Blacks as a curtain raiser for the international to come. It was not to be and we went down 19-3. You can laugh at this if you like but I think one of the reasons we lost was that for the only time I can remember we were kitted out in white socks which made us feel pretty soft as we took the field.

The green patch of grass so dear to my heart: Mansfield Park. (Courtesy: Bob Thomas)

The international at Murrayfield was the following month and Scotland went down by a disappointing 20-6, our only scores being two second-half penalty goals by Andy Irvine. One thing that sticks out in my mind in that match is a great try by Murray Mexted, the All Black No.8 who took a two-handed catch at a short line-out and simply barged his way over. Another is that Graham Mourie, who was again captain on this tour, paid tribute to Scotland by donning the kilt for the official post-match dinner.

It's always an honour and privilege to play against New Zealand All Blacks and I've always been envious of the way they keep on producing world-class players and teams. I've made many good friends out there, none more so than Andy Dalton whom I first met in 1978. He actually invited Val to go over and stay with him and his wife Pip during the 1987 World Cup, but she decided not to go. Other players and friends whose names spring to mind are Gary Knight, Mark Shaw, the great goal-kicking full-back Alan Hewson, the deadly wing duo of Stu Wilson and Bernie Fraser and that prince of scrum-halves Dave Loveridge.

But there are a whole host of great names in a country where sport is king and rugby is No.1. It's amazing that a small country like New Zealand produces so many champions in everything from cricket to athletics. The New Zealand Government, of course, promote sport heavily and if you and your family don't play or participate in some kind of sporting activity then you're pretty well an outcast. I was speaking to a rugby historian in Christchurch when I was last over there and he reckoned that there were more rugby clubs in that town than in the whole of Scotland. So on that basis we don't do too badly when we get the chance to play the All Blacks.

There's a consistency about All Blacks play which is based on their set-up. Everyone from club through to provincial to international status plays in the same manner. The result is that players knit together easily at whichever level they reach.

The basic foundation of the All Blacks success is a forward platform, winning good clean possession from line-out and scrum, getting the ball to quicksilver scrum-halves who in turn release the unending supply of talented backs. This coupled with the famed rucking power of the Blacks makes them a feared team indeed. If you lie on the ball then you're unceremoniously rucked out of the way and I can tell you from personal experience that the New

My elder son Roddy at an early age tries on my cap. Maybe one day he may earn his own.

Zealanders aren't too fussy where they place their feet.

Thanks to Telfer and Grant, I'd say the only country outside the two Islands who nowadays resemble the All Blacks in their desire to ruck must be Scotland.

There was quite a long gap — until February 1980 — before Scotland took the field again, against Ireland at Lansdowne Road. Unfortunately, it was still not long enough to get a winning side together. The selectors took a gamble in picking five new caps and although we were beaten 22-15, some great tries were scored on both sides, including two by David Johnston for Scotland, and there appeared at last to be hope for the future. Amongst the cap debutants in that match was Roy Laidlaw, whom I rate the best scrum-half Scotland has ever had in my time. He's like a Border terrier or, to give him his nickname, a ferret. A great wee guy and an outstanding player.

Our next international was at Murrayfield against France, also in February, and what an astonishing game it was. For me personally it was a disaster. But for Scotland it ended a long sequence without a win.

Andy Irvine was having a bad time with his kicking in the first-half, then he suddenly came good in the second period, ripping up the French defence. We finally won 22-14. But I don't take any credit at all for that — in fact I was sitting watching what was going on for most of the game.

As always with the French, the scrummaging was very hard. I had struck for the ball in the first scrum and while I was still in the hooking position the opposing props Vaqurrin and Paparemborde bore in on me from either side. Something had to give and when the scrum broke up, I went down. I was in pure panic for I felt this awful, searing pain. I was given treatment on the field but at the next scrum it seemed even worse and I had to be helped off with tears in my eyes.

I didn't need a doctor to tell me my ribs had been damaged and all I could do was shake hands with Ken Lawrie of Gala as he took my place for his first cap. After a pain-killing injection I watched the remainder of the game and I was able to attend the official dinner, but I was side-lined for eight weeks.

Of course the injury put me out of any contention for a Lions place and before that kept me out of the teams which lost to Wales in Cardiff and England at Murrayfield. By their 30-18 victory England took not only the Calcutta Cup but the Grand Slam. Despite that loss, though, I was glad to see five of my Scots colleagues picked for the Lions. How I envied them!

There was, however, some consolation for me when I was selected to go on a three-match tour of France in April and May. It was to be a really rugged series of matches and of course I wasn't fully tuned up. But I'm convinced it was that tour, with all the boys mixing so well and trying so hard, that laid the foundations of the 1984 Grand Slam team.

I was really glad to be in on the French connection for I had fretted during my weeks out of the game missing squad sessions. I vowed then I'd never moan about doing three-and-a-half-hour training stints on Sundays. Amongst those also selected for the tour and who were later to appear in the Grand Slam squad of 1984 were Peter Dods, David Johnston, Steve Munro, Roy Laidlaw, Keith Robertson, John Rutherford, Jim Calder and David Leslie.

It was Jim Telfer's first involvement with the squad and for the first time we really trained, not once but twice a day. Jim had a great admiration for New Zealand rugby and had obviously picked up a few tips. He used to hold a rod or stick at a certain height and we had to scrum under it, going in low and looking ahead. Another of his ploys was to get a rucking bag filled with sawdust and make us step over it, planting the left or right foot and providing a platform for the next man up. He was always on about using the knee and shoulder to bump the opposition.

It was undoubtedly Telfer who set the standard for us. Up until then we'd been playing at training. But he had us knocking hell out of each other at the sessions and we've carried on with that under Derrick Grant who, like Jim, is a great admirer of the All Blacks play. It's been tough but it has paid dividends because the rucking we saw from the Grand Slam side was probably the best seen up until then by a Scottish team.

If I wasn't really tuned up by the start of this tour I certainly was by the end. To say it was going to be an austere experience is putting it mildly. For a kick-off, when we gathered at the North British Hotel in Edinburgh we were issued with a hold-all and a pair of grey trousers. There were no special blazers or emblems. I feel that was a bad mistake by the SRU for after all we were going over to represent Scottish rugby as their ambassadors.

I wasn't picked for the first match which was against a French select. And for once I was quite content, for we lost 20-6. However, within three days Telfer had welded us into a decent unit.

We moved to Agen to play a French Barbarians side which turned out to be really the French Grand Slam team of 1975. The day before the game some of the boys wanted to walk into the town just half a mile away. Telfer had other ideas. He wanted them to rest in the afternoon so that they were ready to train again in the evening. When he asked why they wanted to go into town they said they'd like to get some sweets. Said the bold Jim, "Away to your beds." And off he went into town to return with a huge bag of sweets. Somehow, though, I don't think that had been the original thinking behind the boys' request!

YOU'RE A HOOKER, THEN

At one of the training sessions Gerry McGuinness and Gordon Dickson, who both have red hair, and who both have an aversion to too much sun at the best of times, were in trouble because the sun was beating down on us. Poor Gerry at last plucked up courage to hold his hand up like a wee boy at primary school wanting to go to the toilet and asked Jim, "Could I put on some suntan oil and a hat?" Jim muttered for ages after that about it being the first time anyone had left one of his training sessions to put some suntan oil on.

Before the game against the French Barbarians it was Telfer who took the team talk and he certainly wanted us to show aggression. He niggled fellows like big David Gray, who towered over him, calling him useless; he rubbished strong man prop Norrie Rowan for wearing a tee shirt two sizes too small; and he hammered on at George Mackie so much that the normally docile Mackie could stand no more. He swung a hay-maker at Telfer and for the first time on the tour Telfer picked himself up and smiled. He had got through.

In the game itself there was one hilarious moment when the French prop Cholley, who had been a professional boxer, was up against McGuinness. He had obviously been doing something illegal and Gerry swung out at him. Cholley merely put his arms out and held Gerry off. While he kept on swinging gamely, poor Gerry couldn't get near the craggy Frenchman. It could have been mayhem. But it was so much like a clip from a Keystone Kops movie that we, and the French, burst out laughing. Even Cholley grinned and things simmered down.

Without any hesitation I say that was a game we would have won had not the French referee Palmade given a try which wasn't a try to his Barbarian side. The final result was 26-22 and even Telfer seemed quite pleased.

Next we moved to Brive for the third and final game on 3 May. It coincided with my birthday and I got an unexpected present and honour by being appointed skipper for the match, taking over from Roy Laidlaw who was the overall tour captain and who had already played in two games.

It was a niggly kind of game and indeed our second-row forward David Gray, a gentle giant if ever there was one, was warned for punching. The truth was that in the previous two games we had been on the receiving end and when we decided to give the natives some of their own back they just didn't want to know. We came out with an honourable 7-7 draw but again I felt the boys were robbed, for we had scored a perfectly good try in the last minutes which was disallowed. Still, we knew in our hearts that we were the victors and there was champagne in the dressing room after the match. So ended a tour which I'm convinced provided the foundation of a squad destined to produce some vintage rugby over the next five or six years.

My next big moment was at Cardiff at the end of November 1980 when I was picked for a combined Scotland/Ireland team to play England/Wales in a Welsh centenary match. It was a terrific experience and I met Fergus Slattery, the great Irish forward, for the first time. I was young and fit and I thought I could run him into the ground in our training session. But it was, I confess, completely the other way round.

What a fine player, and what a fine constitution these Irish lads had. On our way back to the hotel on the Friday night we stopped for a pint at a Cardiff pub. For me and most of the other lads it was literally one pint for we were aware of the big game ahead. I learned later however that Slats and Willie Duggan had somehow 'accidentally' got locked in at the pub and were forced to down about half-a-dozen pints. It didn't make any difference to their tremendous standard of play and I gathered that was a pretty normal Friday night for them.

The game itself, in front of a crowd of 37,000, was a cracker. Before it started we were all introduced to Her Majesty the Queen and believe me it was quite a thrill.

We started off with seven Scots in the side and when David Irwin was injured Keith Robertson came on to make it eight. Andy Irvine captained our side and Steve Fenwick the opposition. England/Wales, thanks to an injury time try by the great Gareth Davies, who converted it himself, squeezed through by 37-33 just as we were celebrating victory in our hearts. Despite the high score and the fact that a lot of these show games are just spectacular exhibitions, this was a real match. As prop Graham Price, who needed five stitches to an eye cut during the game, commented, "It was hard and competitive."

On 17 January 1981 we took on France at the Parc des Princes but it proved as difficult as usual to win there and we were beaten 16-9. Two aspects I recall about that game were that Jim Renwick had a try disallowed and Andy Irvine, who was captain, set a world record for scoring points in international matches. But as Andy said himself, he'd gladly have given up any record in exchange for a Scots victory.

The following month Scotland's luck, and mine, changed dramatically against Wales at Murrayfield. We started off with a bang, our morale soared and we never looked like being beaten. The score-line was 15-6. It was our first win over the Welsh dragons since 1975 and my first full victory in internationals. During the game I needed three stitches for a cut near the eye but that didn't matter. I'd lasted out the full game on a winning side. There were telegrams from my family and friends waiting for me at the Edinburgh hotel where we held the post-match dinner. What really pleased me most however was when Renwick told me I'd played my best game ever in a Scottish jersey.

Our new found confidence was pricked by England in the next match at Twickenham. The English team shook us by the display of their backs, for until then there was a general impression that while they could usually muster a good pack they had nothing behind it. Well, the theory was proved all wrong on that particular day and England ran out 23-17 winners. The winner's ace was a new stand-off by the name of Huw Davies, while our most popular player was Steve Munro, the Ayr winger who nipped in for two tries.

Probably with the idea of maintaining continuity for the New Zealand tour which Scotland faced in the summer, the selectors named the same side as that which had gone down to England for the final home countries match against Ireland at Murrayfield.

The weather had been extremely bad and the boys were at times sliding about. But we got home by 10-9. Highlight of the afternoon was a try by Bruce Hay. Bold Bruce intercepted a David Irwin pass, tucked the ball under his arm and, chased all the way by Tony Ward, ran 60 yards for the touch down. Now Bruce will admit he is no Seb Coe so it was all the more remarkable that he should pinch that try. Of course the irrepressible Renwick had to have the last word. He cracked, "When you see Bruce running his heart out on TV, it'll just look like a slow motion replay." There's just no pleasing some folks!

Still I was pleased personally. We'd notched up two home wins, there had been the chance to play with the all-time greats in the centenary match at Cardiff and, to end the season, I accepted an invitation to sit on the bench — again at Cardiff — when Wales played a World side. The man who had pipped me for the position of hooker in the World side was Peter Wheeler.

The World XV contained some of the best players going and I was really thrilled to meet them all and made many friends. Amongst those on parade were Andy Haden, Dave Loveridge, Brendan Moon, Jean-Pierre Rives, Mark Ella and Rob Louw, who was one of three South Africans present.

My most enjoyable memory was not of the rugby, although the game was a thriller with Wales winning by 27-23, but of playing a round of golf with Mark Ella. Ella, a little man with a perpetual grin who lived only for rugby, was no mean golfer. He had an eye for the ball and I was playing some pretty Mickey Mouse stuff. But I did make him sit up and take notice with one shot I made with a six iron from about 200 yards off the green. I got the ball to within a foot of the hole, earning the plaudits of Mark. Unfortunately it was the only good shot I played that day. Mark and I have kept in touch ever since.

This, incidentally, was the first rugby match I'd been at where there was a demonstration — because of our three South Africans — and it was a bit scary. However, fortunately, there was no violence and everything went smoothly.

Yes, it had been a good season for me, capped by the fact that I was told I was in the squad to tour New Zealand in May and June of 1981. Tour manager was Ken Smith, a Border farmer and ex-British Lion who was popular with the boys, coach was Jim Telfer and captain Andy Irvine. So we had a fine trio at the top and everyone in the party looked forward to visiting what I regard as the best rugby-playing country in the world.

Chapter 9

LIFE IN THE LAND OF THE LONG WHITE CLOUD

PREPARATIONS were well in hand long before our season finished for our eight-match tour of New Zealand in May and June of 1981. When I saw the itinerary I realised just how much planning goes into a major tour — fixing up flights, hotels, training grounds, official receptions, and now and again a wee game of rugby. I certainly take my hat off to all the administrators who have the task of making a tour trouble-free.

On 3 May, my 26th birthday, I was taking part in a gruelling squad session under Jim Telfer at Murrayfield instead of tucking into a birthday cake. It turned out to be a fateful session for one of the boys, John Beattie, the big No.8 who at the time was playing for Heriot's.

One of Telfer's ploys after the session was officially over was to lob the ball high into the air and nominate a player to catch it, then run at a bunch of the boys down the pitch. Big John grabbed the ball OK and made a run. Unfortunately for him Iain 'The Bear' Milne was the first guy he encountered. John went in to try and knock The Bear off balance, but Iain lowered his shoulder and the next thing we knew Beattie was writhing in agony on the ground. He had to be stretchered off and taken to hospital with a fractured knee cap, which of course needed an operation and kept him out of the tour.

It was a sad moment for everyone because we had all soldiered on together and here was John missing out on an extremely important chance to further his career. The original No.8 choices, in fact, had been Beattie and Peter Lillington of Durham University who also called off because of exams.

Sad though it was, John's injury was one of those things you must expect in rugby. No one was to blame and certainly not The Bear or coach Telfer. Better than any of us Telfer knew just how tough it was going to be the moment we arrived in New Zealand and he had to get the squad in top physical trim while of course he was desperate to incorporate some of the New Zealand style of play into our own strategy. It's rather like preparing soldiers for an important battle. At some stage or other you have to use live bullets and grenades and inevitably someone gets hurt. We were lucky in being able to call on Iain Paxton of Selkirk as a replacement for John. In height and weight Iain was an almost perfect clone of Beattie's so we lost no height in the line-out.

The following week we got all our tour gear — blazer, flannels, hold-all, etc. — and it was just like a good Christmas day with the SRU as Santa Claus. I spent most of my spare time in the next few days getting the garden in trim and then, on 19 May, a mini-bus with some of the boys on board stopped at the house. I had a bit of a lump in my throat saying goodbye to Val and Roddy. The wee fellow expected me home as usual that night but we were off for six weeks.

I didn't have much time to brood however. Once we had left London and were *en route* for Singapore, it was up to Jim Calder and myself to work out rooming arrangements for the tour. That took us most of the journey. We were anxious not to have anyone rooming twice with the same player. I'm a great believer in everyone mixing and getting to know each other. The last thing you want are cliques.

On arrival at Singapore we were all feeling tired and hungry and jet-lag was setting in. However we were up bright and early next morning, looking forward to a long, lazy day until our plane left at night. We reckoned without Telfer. By 11 a.m. we were out at a training ground. The weather was so hot and humid that you were gasping for breath even without exerting yourself. It was so bad that Tom Smith, who is a huge guy of six feet eight inches, actually collapsed.

I've never been so glad to get back to a hotel and have a beer or two in the bar, even though the liquid just seemed to run through your pores. We brightened up in the afternoon when we had the chance to buy some duty-free goods before jetting off to Auckland.

On arrival there we headed by bus to our first training camp at Taumarunui, some three hours' drive away, where we were greeted by a fierce-looking Maori warrior complete with spear and grass skirt. All of us unsophisticated blokes took a dim view of it when he danced up threateningly and stuck out his tongue. Fortunately someone knew that this was the traditional Maori welcome and an international incident was averted. After the gift of a fern which made us honoured guests we were escorted into the Maori meeting hut, met the elders and were then entertained to some great Maori singing.

Next morning it was misty but some of the old hands explained that meant it would be a fine sunny day soon. We were all feeling good — it was one of those moments you were so glad to be alive — and we all tucked into a hearty breakfast. That was a big mistake.

You've guessed it. Task-master Telfer was at us again, anxious not to waste any time, and within half-an-hour we were on the training pitch. Fifteen minutes later we were all minus our breakfasts. We had a two-and-a-half-hour slog before Jim called it off for lunch. But as we heaved a collective sigh of relief he told us to keep our kit on as we were going out again in the afternoon. This time we had 90 minutes of solid scrummaging and by the time we were released all we wanted was to soak in a bath to try and get out the aches and pains. It was a gey tired bunch of rugby men who crawled between the sheets that night, far too worn out to get up to any mischief. On a more serious note, Roy Laidlaw and Andy Irvine picked up groin injuries that day and never really shook them off for the remainder of the tour.

Before the first game against King Country, coached by the great Colin Meads, we did get a day's break. Some of us took a trip on jet boats but the boys who really enjoyed themselves went fishing in a cruiser. The owner simply put a net over the side, anchored the boat and escorted the boys downstairs to imbibe cans of lager. When they hauled the net up at the end of an enjoyable day they found one fish. But it was voted a very successful outing!

I missed the first game, for Ken Lawrie played as hooker. The Scots did well in winning by 39-13 at Taumarunui. It was here that

Substitute Laidlaw gets the ball from Jim Calder. David Leslie and Norrie Rowan look on, against Wellington, 1981.

we first realised the strength of the anti-apartheid movement in New Zealand. South Africa were due to follow us in July — in fact they had postponed their tour from May which let us into that slot — and demonstrators were out to force the Government to stop the Springboks. In case of trouble the floodlights at the ground where we played were kept on all night and patrols were on duty, but fortunately the match passed off without incident.

However, you can judge just how seriously the authorities regarded the strength of feeling amongst the anti-South African demonstrators by the fact that we were given armed bodyguards. We soon made friends with our 'minders' and I recall that some of the boys, including myself, were asked home by one of them. He had a jacuzzi in his back garden and for the first and only time I sat in an open-air jacuzzi in the middle of winter.

On to Wellington where we met the Prime Minister, 'Piggy' Muldoon. Despite his flamboyant reputation he was very polite and rather quiet when we met him. Of course that could have been because a general election was looming up and also because the anti-apartheid lobby was causing headaches to the men in power.

Before the game at the Athletic Park pitch on 30 May we learned that one of Wellington's most respected players and later coach, Al Keowen, had died. His brother George had been a teacher in Hawick and even now the local primary schools play for the George Keowen trophy.

The strength of the Wellingston side can be measured from the fact that they had players like Murray Mexted and Jamie Salmon on duty and we went down by 19-15, most of the damage being caused by that famous All Black Bernie Fraser who scored two splendid tries. Unfortunately for him, and us, our scrum-half that day, Gordon Hunter, sustained a fractured cheekbone so Roy Laidlaw had to come on as replacement although he was still suffering from his groin injury. An SOS was sent home by the management to fly out Alan Lawson who wrapped up his business affairs and joined us as soon as he could.

Our next match was in Masterton against Brian Lochore's side, Wairarapa Bush, and to our delight we won by 32-9. That game is memorable for the fact that there was brawling amongst the spectators, some of whom spilled on to the pitch during the course of the game.

On our travels once more, this time to rugby-mad Christchurch to take on Canterbury. I wasn't too surprised to hear that there are more rugby sides in the area than in the whole of Scotland . . . no wonder the All Blacks are so good. As a bit of light relief before we took on our latest opponents in front of a 25,000 crowd, some of the boys went racing. The Bear, who likes a flutter, collected a couple of quid from each of us . . . and by the second race had lost the lot. A good job for him that he's built on such impressive lines.

The game itself, played on a dark but mainly dry day, was something to cherish. It proved that we had by now moulded into a real team. Canterbury had a host of names destined to become famous, such as Wayne Smith, John Ashworth and Robbie Deans, the latter no relation but like a lot of New Zealanders he claims to have a Scottish connection.

We scored wonderful tries through the swift Steve Munro and a great interception by Laidlaw, four penalty goals by Peter Dods and a drop goal by John Rutherford. Canterbury fought back but too late and we ran out winners by 23-12. I had the honour of being picked as man of the match. However I put that one down to The Bear. He tied up his opposite prop, John Ashworth, reputed to be one of the strongest men in the world in that position, so well that I was able to nick four tight-heads. I made sure Iain got a dram out of the bottle of whisky which was handed over as my prize.

Our last game before the first Test was at Ashburton against Mid-Canterbury. For once I was glad not to be picked, for my ear had started aching the night before the match. I tried pain killers prescribed by the team doctor but they didn't really work and I was up at six o'clock in the morning playing pool by myself because I couldn't sleep.

I sat on the bench to see Scotland winning by the same margin, 23-12, as they had done in the previous fixture. Unfortunately Derek White suffered torn ligaments and that ended his tour. Lillington, who had now finished his exams, was sent for. A lovely try by Lawson, who had only arrived in the country a couple of days before, showed the class of the scrum-half.

My ear was still so painful that I was told not to travel by air to Dunedin with the rest of the boys for the first Test but to go by car. So I finished up with a couple of Scots journalists, Bill McMurtrie of the *Glasgow Herald* and Norman Mair of the *Scotsman*, and, apart from the ear, had an enjoyable trip. Once in Dunedin I attended a hospital clinic where the trouble was diagnosed as a boil which had burst inside the ear. It required a minor operation but it was well worth it to get relief.

Before that of course I had been driven into the town just in time for training. I was beginning to think that for this particular tour it had been a waste of time to pack anything other than my track suit and other training kit.

At Dunedin we were joined by Peter Lillington who was sitting in the team coach, in the driver's seat, when we boarded from yet one more training stint. That of course was the excuse Jim Renwick needed to say, "Drive on." "But I'm with the Scottish squad," protested Peter. "My name is Lillington." Of course Jim knew that but he just retorted in his best Border accent, "And whae the hell's Lillington?"

Dunedin is one of those places that is more Scottish and proud of it than any other town in New Zealand. Even the streets had familiar names — Princes Street, George Street and so on reminded me of Edinburgh. On Saturday 13 June the big day arrived — the

Test against the most powerful rugby nation in the world at that time. Back home in Hawick it also happened to be the Common Riding, a festival unique to Border towns. I reckoned we Hawick lads in the party needed to do something to celebrate and a win over the Blacks would do very nicely.

The Carisbrook ground was packed with 31,000 spectators and there were quite a few St Andrew's Cross flags being waved by descendants of Scots. It was a first cap for Iain Paxton and he was a wee bit overwhelmed. The Blacks for once were without their famous all-black strip to avoid confusion, so they wore white which, funnily enough, made them look smaller than usual, while we were in the proud blue of Scotland.

We attacked from the start but some of the stuffing was knocked out of us when Munro crossed for what he still maintains was a perfectly good try, which the Aussie referee Dick Byres refused. Worse was to come when, despite the fact that we won the ball OK in a scrum the astute Dave Loveridge, the All Blacks scrum-half, dived on it as it crossed our line to touch down a perfectly good try. The killer blow was yet another try by that great winger Stu Wilson.

But in the 69th minute came a moment I still cherish. A badly tapped ball from an All Blacks line-out allowed Paxton to kick ahead. I followed up in support, got the ball and managed to dodge Wilson then outpace the New Zealand defence to touch down a try. It was my first international try in 16 appearances for Scotland and what made it even sweeter was that it was the first try scored by a Scottish touring side against the New Zealanders. I tell you as I walked back to the centre line with Paxton I felt about ten feet tall.

Unfortunately despite several near misses by David Leslie, Andy Irvine and the flying Munro that was the only score we had. A penalty goal by Alan Hewson the full-back tied it up 11-4 for the Blacks. They were, however, the first to admit that in many respects they had been fortunate and certainly morale in the Scottish camp was still high despite that defeat and I, in particular, had plenty to celebrate as I thought of the Common Riding jollifications back home.

At the official dinner that night the All Blacks were pretty subdued at first. They knew they had been in a game. But we Scots were so used to being the bridesmaids on these big occasions that we were able to shrug off our disappointment at not winning. I must say here that in all the time I've been associated with the

Shopping in Auckland before the last Test v New Zealand on 1981 tour. We were no puppets on that tour.

Scottish squad everyone has always played to their best and we've never been a dirty side. Long may that continue. Anyway we soon got the party spirit going and even Bernie Fraser, not noted as the most affable player in the world, took us to his heart. A lot of friendships were made that night and many of them continue to this day.

We were now into the closing stages of the tour with two games to go, including the second Test. First of all we had to deal with Marlborough at Blenheim, where the pre-match training was as hard as one would expect but now didn't seem so bad because, thanks to Jim Telfer, we were all so fit.

However, poor Steve Munro went down with 'flu at Blenheim on his birthday and the boys clubbed together to present him with a cake and card. He was sharing a room with Bruce Hay and, being ill, he didn't present his usual immaculate appearance. Indeed his hair was so tousled that he was promptly called Oor Wullie after a character in the *Sunday Post*, while his room-mate had his nickname of the Flying Gut changed to Fat Bob, another of the characters.

The night we arrived we gathered in the bar for a few cans of beer and played a game of forfeits. It included Andy Irvine having to pretend to be an SAS officer and somersaulting into the bar making the appropriate noises as he "attacked"! Although it may sound daft to some people I've always found that these crazy things allow the players to relax and mix, and if you mix well then it's good for the team.

We were now on song for the second Test and made light work of beating Marlborough by 38-9. Then it was on to Auckland for the final hurdle.

As usual we had a hard training session on the Thursday before the Test and then we practised scrummaging. There was a scrummaging machine which the training ground attendant wheeled out of a shed on two rails which were in a sand-pit. Then he said the All Blacks had earlier that day used the same machine, set at the same pressure. From the look he gave us it was obvious he didn't think we had a hope in hell of moving the machine. It was difficult because you had to stand in the sand and get the maximum shove on. Well, I'm glad to say we proved the old boy wrong. With our first scrum we nearly pushed the machine back through the shed. He couldn't believe his eyes, checked the pressure and raised it again. Later he said that our first shove had been just as good as the All Blacks' best shunt and they had taken 15 minutes to warm up enough to do that. Our spirits soared. We knew that we could out-scrummage the famous Blacks pack.

Next day was a bit of an anti-climax. We expected the usual light session and Press conference. But Jim kept driving away until I think even he realised he was flogging a dead horse. The boys were thinking of what presents they could take home to their wives and kids and it wasn't the right time to ask for more blood and sweat when we knew that would be demanded the following day.

That following day, 20 June, marked Jim Renwick's 41st cap, at that time a new record for a Hawick player. Jim had overtaken Hugh McLeod, the distinguished prop and now a Hawick official, who was known as the Abbot. As his team-mates, Alan Tomes and I bought Jim a little goblet and had it inscribed "Hawick's new Abbot". Mind you, I don't think anyone who knows Jim could imagine him in a priest's habit.

It was that morning when I picked up a national newspaper that

I began to understand how highly rated Andy Irvine was in New Zealand. There was a quarter-page advert on what was to happen before the big game. On one side was a picture of the All Black skipper Graham Mourie, on the other a picture of Andy. The caption under Mourie's picture merely said it was his final appearance in 1981. Under Andy's it read, "This is possibly your last chance to see this legend." What an honour for an 'outsider' in a country acknowledged as the world leader in the sport.

The Test was played at Eden Park in front of a 40,000 crowd. By the interval we were only down 10-6, with Bruce Hay touching down a try which Irvine converted in answer to two Stu Wilson tries, one converted by Alan Hewson. But the second-half began badly, with Mourie and Hewson getting tries, before two penalty goals by Irvine and a Renwick drop goal gave us heart. However the bad luck which had dogged us in the big matches on this tour continued when David Leslie, Roy Laidlaw and Jim Calder all looked about to score. Indeed Jim was over the line but was hauled back for an earlier infringement.

The real sickener for us, however, was when Munro intercepted 60 yards from the All Blacks' line but with no one to stop him. Normally it would have been like stealing candy from a blind man, but Steve hadn't recovered from his bout of flu and Bernie Fraser caught and nailed him. After that the heads were down and the Blacks cut loose in the last quarter, winning by 40-15. The score doesn't reflect the way the game was played and more than once I thought we would win it. However the tour had done a tremendous lot for all of us and set the pattern for the type of play we had been aiming for.

It was party time at the conclusion of the tour, with the New Zealand Rugby Union giving us a marvellous farewell following the official dinner the night before.

There was only one sour note about our journey back home. We had changed from a delightful New Zealand aircraft to a British Airways plane at Los Angeles. One of the boys politely asked how long the flight to Heathrow would take. "Too long with you lot," the stewardess replied frostily. Somehow by the end of our journey I think she regretted making that remark, which was not made in fun.

We arrived in Edinburgh to a good reception from the Press and Ken Smith praised us for being good ambassadors. Jim Telfer as

Dunedin in 1st Test 1981. Dave Loveridge scores that sneaky try.

usual wanted to see harder matches between the top players and made his views known by saying, "These boys have been out on tour, getting hardened up. There's no point in them coming away from New Zealand to play meaningless matches here." Poor Derek White arrived home with his leg in plaster, but Gordon Hunter was recovering rapidly from his cheekbone break.

From my point of view it was great to see Val and Roddy again. It must be hell to be left alone for six weeks with a young child while your husband is off on what is really an extended holiday with good company and always something new happening. Because of the tour I couldn't manage to get a full summer holiday but the three of us had a very welcome long weekend.

Chapter 10

TEST WIN IN AUSSIE LAND

IT WAS a flying, and historic, start to season 1981/82. In September, having beaten Edinburgh and the South, Romania met Scotland in an international at Murrayfield for the first time ever. Before the game John Rutherford was ruled out because of a leg injury which caused him to break down in training, and Ron Wilson of London Scottish, who hadn't been at the squad session, had to be whistled up. We knew the Iron Curtain boys would be a bit of a handful, and so it proved. However Andy Irvine had one of his glory days and he banged over four penalty goals to two by Ion Constantin to win us the match 12-6.

It seemed we were entertaining the world that season, for just before Christmas the touring Australians also came to Murrayfield. We won the match by 24-15, with Irvine again doing his stuff, kicking five penalty goals and converting a Jim Renwick try, and with Rutherford popping over a drop goal. But the match will be remembered more for an amazing incident when Tony Shaw, the Aussie captain, stretched lock Bill Cuthbertson out on the Murrayfield turf with a full-blooded right to the jaw. English referee Roger Quittenton merely warned Shaw and awarded a penalty to Scotland, but the Australian skipper was desperately lucky not to walk.

Bill told me what happened later. Shaw had queried every decision given by the ref, until Bill couldn't stand it any longer and said, "Shut up. Let's get on with the game." Shaw's response was quick and to the point! Quittenton's excuse for not sending Shaw off was that he hadn't been previously warned and the blow wasn't premeditated.

Still we'd won the match and that set us up for the season to come. I also remember that game personally for a tackle I made on Andrew Slack which nearly stopped him from scoring. I opened my knee on a corner flag in completing the tackle and Slack was kind enough to seek me out after the game to have a beer and a chat. A promising young winger, Roger Baird, also earned his first Scottish cap in the fixture.

Following that match I was picked as reserve for the Barbarians who were to play the Aussies in Cardiff in their final tour appearance. That was in January 1982 and I travelled down with the rest of the Scottish contingent — Irvine, Baird, Roy Laidlaw and Iain Milne.

When we arrived we noticed a bit of snow around but retired to bed early and didn't think much about it. Next day however the snow was around 18 inches and lying and eventually the game was called off. We had hired a car at Heathrow and there seemed no chance at all of getting back there so we decided to drive home up the motorway. There were signs saying it was closed but we drove on anyway with Andy at the wheel. Every now and again we passengers had to get out and shove the car through snowdrifts. It was so bad at one time that Andy didn't dare stop and poor Roger was left to run and catch us, throwing himself into the open door very breathless.

I got into Hawick about 4.30 a.m. and then did some training later in the morning. I think the only person who was quite pleased with the whole affair was Val. It's the only time I can remember shopping with her in Hawick High Street on a Saturday afternoon during the season!

However, on to sterner things, and we opened the Five Nations campaign at Murrayfield against the Auld Enemy, England, who were tipped to win the Grand Slam. Well, the role of underdogs suits Scotland. It seemed that we were going to lose when we were 9-6 down. Prop Colin Smart however gave away a penalty with a push on Iain Paxton and up stepped that man Irvine to kick a 57-yarder which drew the game. It was his second penalty of the match, the other score being a Rutherford drop goal.

Our luck ran out in windy Dublin in February, with Ollie Campbell getting all his country's 21 points to our 12 and clinching the Triple Crown for Ireland for the first time in 33 years. We were continually lectured by the Welsh referee Clive Norling during that match and the guy I felt sorry for was Eric Paxton who was gaining his first Scottish cap. By the time Norling had niggled at us time after time poor Eric was scared to move in case he gave an offside penalty away.

Before our next international we in Hawick had a small score to settle with Gala, who at the time were champions.

The rivalry between the two clubs — indeed the two towns — is something to marvel at. There are only 20 miles between the two but it might as well be America versus Russia. Coach Derrick Grant tried to make us supermen in the space of a week. Not even squad training for the internationals can match the build-up for this particular fixture in the Borders.

On the Thursday night everything seemed to be falling into place and after soaking out some of the bruising we sat around the clubhouse discussing tactics . . . and carefully keeping out of Derrick's way. Friday was a little bit like waiting to go over the top. Saturday morning and the kit was packed hours before the match was due to kick off. Val, and I'm sure all the other players' wives in the town, were glad to see the back of us.

This particular encounter in February 1982 lived up to all its promise. We were leading 9-3 at the interval. Then one of our boys, Keith Murray, had to go off with a bad shoulder injury. We soldiered on with 14 men, but Gala gradually got a grip on things and when stand-off Jimmy Maitland dropped a goal two minutes into injury time even I thought it was all over. But there was just time for us to get a penalty award for handling by Gala. The ice-cool Jim Renwick scrubbed away at his thinning hair as he always did on these occasions, put down his head, followed through and we had won the game by 12-10. After that we could hardly do any other but go on to take the championship title . . . which we did.

Almost immediately it was back to the Five Nations championship, with France visitors to Murrayfield. I think we all felt we'd been niggled out of our stride against Ireland and we had something to prove to ourselves. So we threw caution to the winds as we felt the French, who are not great travellers, begin to show signs of

Referee. it's a perfectly good try! It wasn't. A forward pass against France, 1982.

indiscipline and to bicker amongst themselves. By the end we had outlasted and outclassed them in every part of the game and we should really have won by more than 16-7. Irvine, who was captain, said he thought the pack had played as well as any he'd seen in ten years. Andy himself didn't do badly, mind you. He kicked three penalty goals, Renwick dropped a goal and Rutherford touched down a try.

So it was on to the final game of the international season, against Wales in Cardiff. . . always a hard one. But our morale was high and we felt pretty good. We stayed at the St Pierre Golf and Country Club about 40 miles outside Cardiff. It was ideal for relaxing and training and the only thing which spoiled our enjoyment was that Keith Robertson went down with tonsilitis. Jim Pollock of Gosforth was called in. He was a very competent player and quickly slotted into the squad.

The game was to prove that our confidence in ourselves, and in Pollock, was not misplaced. Remember the Welsh hadn't lost a game on their home pitch since 1968. As expected, they came roaring out at us like a bunch of lions looking for a meal of Christians. But we didn't turn the other cheek, I'm afraid. We knew the referee was Jean-Pierre Bonnet and, like all French refs, he was in favour of letting a match flow. So we decided to oblige him.

This fixture probably spelled the end of a brilliant career for Gareth Davies; it certainly re-launched Scotland as a good attacking, running side. It was Davies who, early on, decided to go for a corner kick. But the ball bounced over the head of Roger Baird who was in his own 25. He had time to gather it, then everyone waited for him to kick into touch as most wingers would have done. Instead Baird shimmied past a player, passed to Iain Paxton and the big fellow took off like a French forward. He was felled but had time to pass to Alan Tomes who made ground with Jim Calder and myself in support. The pass went out to Jim and we were over for a glory try.

In the move Paxton was hurt and had to be replaced by Gordon Dickson. However the Scots felt in their bones that they had the winning of the match and never faltered. We finished up with a victory of 34-18. It was the biggest win ever for Scotland in Wales and the greatest margin the Welsh had ever been beaten by at their headquarters. Our try scorers that day were Calder, Pollock, White, Renwick and Johnston. Renwick and Irvine had drop goals and the latter kicked four conversions. The Welsh skipper Butler got their only try which Gwyn Evans, the full-back, converted to add to his four penalty goals. It was champagne for dinner that night and sore heads in the morning. But, boyo, it was certainly worth it.

While a lot of the boys were able to go off for a well-earned rest at the end of the home season, those of us picked for the summer Australian tour which consisted of nine matches, including two Tests, stayed in training. After a long hard season you'll realise that it's not much fun sweating it out until June and July. However the lure of an overseas tour is always strong and we left London bound for Brisbane in high spirits.

When we got there we had a relaxed workout — an indication that Jim Telfer was now listening to the senior players and not treating them like raw recruits. But the tour nearly started with a disaster. We had gone down to the beach which is nowhere like Portobello and is aptly called Surfers' Paradise. It was here that one of the lads

They shall not pass. But if they do Jacques Cousteau will stop them.

damn nearly ended in paradise. The sea plunged steeply from the beach and the strength of the surf was so strong that it could drag you in. We had been warned of the dangers and told to hold a hand up if we got into difficulties. Anyway we were larking around when we spotted Bill Cuthbertson with his hand up.

He's a great guy Bill and a bit of a joker and at first we thought he was kidding. Then we saw he really was in trouble. Jim Calder, who was nearest, swam to help him and Bill pushed him under the sea. As Jim choked and eventually got to the beach Alan Tomes and Derek White dived to the rescue. In the end we were relieved to see Bill hauled out of the water. It was only then he confessed he couldn't swim, but he had been hauled in by the suction of the tide.

He was promptly christened Jacques Cousteau, but there's no doubt it could have been a very serious business. And for all of you who wonder about the tales of drowning men . . . yes, Bill swears the whole of his past life flashed in front of him as if it were on a TV video.

It gives you some idea of the distances in Australia that our first game at Mount Isa meant a 1,000-mile journey to play Queensland County. As part of the official activities we were invited down the local copper mine. Our guide got chatting and mentioned his wife had been a nurse in Edinburgh. Then I discovered she had helped in the birth of Roddy back in 1979. So the couple were made welcome in the team hotel that night and of course I proudly displayed pictures of young Roddy.

I was on the bench for that game and I remember the pitch was so hard that the firemen were hosing it down while an old Scots lady we met after the match, which we won, complained about the cold. It was only 86 degrees!

Back we flew to Brisbane for our next match against Queensland, the main side in the district. We didn't do too well, coming off beaten by 18-7.

Then it was down to Sydney where we had an unexpectedly long gap before our next match — against Sydney on the Saturday. We had time for a bit of social life, including a memorable cruise in the harbour and also some tough training which seemed to go well. But we played on the cricket ground — and without making excuses, that's a heck of a lot different from a normal rugby pitch — and finished up with a 22-13 defeat.

Everyone was on a 'downer' after that result. Sometimes a downer can hit an individual player, if perhaps his wife isn't coping too well at home, but sometimes it hits an entire team and that can really mar any tour. We badly needed a boost. And we went to Melbourne to get it. It rained and rained and rained just like home . . . and we began to feel better.

For the match itself against Melbourne it was 'Cousteau' Cuthbertson who was made captain. A wonderful character, Bill has one of the best amateur singing voices I've heard. He led the boys — I was on the bench — to a 38-3 win and it was just the result we had all wanted to get us back on the rails.

That was proved when we returned to Sydney to play New South Wales, again on the cricket ground. But this time it was a different story. We had a great 31-17 win in which both The Bear and myself picked up tries. It was just the tonic we wanted before the first Test in eight days' time.

Before that we headed for a little town called Singleton and passed through Hunter Valley which is famed for its Tyrell wines. We stopped for a wine tasting, followed by a barbecue lunch, followed by wine and wine. It was an ideal opportunity to let our hair down — those of us who had any — and it was very enjoyable.

No staying up late that night but we were up and about in the morning looking for breakfast. There wasn't any. They had some kind of complicated system in the chalets where we were housed which meant you asked the previous night for what you wanted and it was put in a little hatch which you opened from your room at the designated time. As no one had told us of this arrangement we went hungry.

In Singleton the night life revolved round the local working men's club to which we were invited. When we got there we were amazed to find rows and rows of gaming machines . . . the Aussies certainly like to gamble.

As the night wore on Cousteau Cuthbertson acted as choirmaster while we sang songs like *Flower of Scotland* and ended up with *Little Old Wine Drinker Me*. Bill, who was on stage, was having a whale of a time and when we sat down he continued singing. He's got a wonderful voice and everyone was spellbound. When at last he ended his concert it was to a standing ovation from the local farmers and their wives. What an entertainer . . . and what a good lock forward.

On the Thursday we played New South Wales Country and won by 44-3, another confidence booster. I know Americans celebrate on 4 July and I was hoping Scots would too, for that was the date of the Test at Brisbane. We did, in style, by winning 12-7.

Now it's something special to win away from home at any time but to win in the southern hemisphere is quite wonderful. We were level at the interval, thanks to a Rutherford drop goal, Hawker getting an Aussie penalty. Then at a scrum on the Australian line I nicked one against the head, Laidlaw put Robertson off for a try on the blind side and Irvine landed a difficult conversion. Hawker scored the try of the match to leave just a couple of points in it. Then Tony Shaw, who seemed to have something against Scots, was foolish enough to punch me on the jaw. Irvine stepped up to complete the scoring.

I took a great deal of personal satisfaction out of the win, for Australian coach Bob Templeton picked me out as man of the match. He said, "Deans is the best outfield hooker playing in world rugby today. His speed and opportunist play is a delight to watch. He has the qualities to become an all-time great." I think Bob was laying it on a bit, but it was nice to get such praise from such an influential figure.

One memory I'll retain from that match was, when we were 9-7 up, seeing a kilted Scotsman on the dead-ball line doing a Highland fling. About 2,000 irate Aussies were throwing beer cans at him but he couldn't care less, his team were winning. Scots always rally round their ain no matter where they go!

We celebrated a bit, as you can imagine, but then girded our loins for the final provincial game at Canberra against Australian Capital Territories, in which we ran out 22-4 winners.

Back to Sydney for the second Test and last match of the tour. When we took the field the heavens opened. Iain Paxton had to go off with a twisted back muscle early in the second-half to be replaced by his namesake Eric Paxton. Wee Roy Laidlaw got a kick on the head and had blurred vision. But the real killer was that we were penalised so often and Paul McLean was so good with his kicks in the miserable conditions that we were hardly in the hunt.

Having said all that there's no doubt the Australians earned their 33-9 win. They had done their homework well and they were determined to overcome us at any cost. It would have been nice to end up winning two Tests but at least we had shown that Scotland were no pushovers and it's not very often any side can go Down Under and come back with even a share of the spoils. Indeed that first win in the southern hemisphere goes down in the history books.

So it was back home and a few weeks off to get the garden in trim before reporting to Mansfield Park for yet another season, at the end of which lay the glittering prize of a place in the British Lions squad to New Zealand.

Chapter 11

VICTORY MAKES YOU ILL

THERE was an early representative start for season 1982/83 with Fiji touring in Scotland. They were hammered 47-12 by Edinburgh in a midweek match before coming down to Mansfield Park to be beaten 23-17 by South of Scotland. Then the Anglos had a 29-19 victory at Hughenden, so it was a pretty desperate Fijian side that faced a Scotland XV at Murrayfield on 25 September 1982. They crashed to a 32-12 defeat, but despite the fact that they had lost all four games in Scotland I must say that the Fijians were a delight to watch when they ran and every man was a ball player.

The Fijian manager Paulu Cavu, a very popular man, said that despite the defeats morale was still high in the Fijian ranks. And he was honest enough to say, "Everyone here has overrated us. There have been big strides in the way the game is played in Britain over the past ten years and we are here to learn."

It gives you some idea of the pace the match was played at that Peter Dods, at that time still to become an international, and who indeed was the only uncapped player in the Scotland side, said feelingly, "I've never run as much in a game. I thought I'd die in the first 20 minutes." Fortunately for Scotland he didn't and indeed scored 17 of our points.

On my own domestic front Val was told to expect our second baby in May or June and we both knew that I might well be away with the Lions at the time. She was having a hard time of it and it put a bit of a strain on both of us ... but particularly her.

Before the first of the Five Nations games, against Ireland on 15 January, South entertained another touring side, Wellington of New Zealand. We won 24-6 but the whole game was spoiled by the ordering off of two of the tourists, Brian McGrattan and Tu Wyllie. The New Zealand players were sent off by Irish referee Harry O'Connor as the match boiled over in the second-half. McGrattan was sent off for throwing a punch and Wyllie for a dangerous high tackle.

Their manager Brian Frederickson was incensed, particularly at McGrattan's dismissal. "Sure he threw a punch," he admitted, "but it didn't even connect." At a disciplinary hearing following the game Wyllie was given two weeks' suspension and McGrattan one. But that meant both were unable to play in their final tour match against Devon and Cornwall — a sad ending to their Scottish visit.

Personally, I thought the Wellington winger Bernie Fraser was extremely lucky not to join his two clubmates on the way to an early bath. He twice stopped Keith Robertson with straight arm tackles. The referee had his whistle in his mouth and an ordering-off was a certainty. But Bernie suddenly slumped to the ground — I'm sure he was faking — and the referee hesitated until he 'came to' and we were awarded a penalty.

So on to Ireland at Murrayfield. That proved disappointing, for the team they nicknamed "Dad's Army" because of the number of veterans playing edged us out by 15-13, with Ollie Campbell getting 11 points.

After that of course we were given no chance against France in Paris. But Scotland always do best when they're labelled no-hopers and we put on a very good performance despite the fact that in the end we were beaten 19-15. Two players stand out in my memory of that particular match — Bryan Gossman, who was making only his second Scotland appearance at stand-off, and Jean-Pierre Rives, the French flanker and skipper.

Rives was the pin-up boy of French rugby with his mane of blond hair and film star good looks and he was playing his 40th game for his country, his 22nd as captain. He was always a tough cookie, Rives, and one of his compatriots, Daniel Revallier, put it very nicely when he said, "You follow Rives because where he is, the ball is." Well,

The lengths I'll go to supply my buddy with good ball. (Courtesy: Bob Thomas)

Scotland wasn't going to make life easy for Rives, even if it was his 40th appearance in a French jersey. Most folk sat back to wait for the massacre. But in fact we kept plugging on hopefully to the end with a great chance of creating the surprise of the decade.

Peter Dods opened the scoring for us with a penalty goal. Full-back Serge Blanco squared the scores with a similar kick. Then we had a purple passage with John Beattie driving from a scrum pick-up. I carried on the move, passed to Roy Laidlaw and he sent Keith Robertson in for a try which Dods converted.

Gossman, whose only previous appearance in a Scottish strip had

114

been against Wales in 1980, was playing as if he'd never been out of the team and from a free kick Laidlaw put him in possession to allow him to drop a goal. The French looked rattled but before we could land the killer punch that man Serge Blanco eased the pressure on his side with another penalty goal. Just on the interval the French got a vital score with Patrick Esteve crossing our line for Blanco to convert and make it 12-12.

But Scotland and Gossman weren't finished and the stand-off dropped his second goal of the game only to see Blanco, in first-half injury time, kick a penalty which made it 15-15 at the interval and still anyone's game.

France were penalised for offside in the second-half but Dods couldn't manage the resulting penalty and in the 33rd minute of the half Esteve — what a winger — scored an unconverted try. We had one chance left and passed up the idea of going for a penalty goal in an attempt to score a try. The French defence, though, held firm.

Much to my dismay we were made favourites against Wales at Murrayfield and not so surprisingly we lost by the same margin as we had in Paris. We put in a spirited finish but by that time the match had slipped away. The match was notable for the fact that Jim Renwick was celebrating his 50th cap and he did it in style with a try near the end. Dods converted that one and kicked three penalty goals. But as Roy Laidlaw said, "Against Ireland I thought we should have won. Against France I thought we might have won. But this time when we did get going it was far too late."

Changes were made for the final Five Nations match against England at Twickenham and perhaps most significantly these included switching the captaincy from Roy Laidlaw to Jim Aitken. Now Roy is a marvellous player but I had thought myself that the burden of captaincy had weighed heavily on him and affected his own high standard of play.

We had a new cap in Tom Smith, a basketball internationalist, who, it was hoped, would add a new dimension to our line-out play and John Rutherford was back to join his old pal Laidlaw in the half-backs. Despite all that, of course, the harsh fact remained that we hadn't won at the English headquarters since 1971.

I didn't think I'd even make the game for a while. I was sharing a room with The Bear and I felt terribly sick — so much so that I had to ask the doc for something to ease my stomach pains which at first I

The bear asks for a racing tip.

had put down to nerves. However I managed to train on Friday and get to Twickenham on Saturday.

The rest is history. Big Smith scored a try from the line-out and we ran out 22-12 winners. To mark the occasion I was violently sick when we got off the pitch. I found out later that The Bear had just recovered from a stomach bug and I must have caught it. However illness couldn't hide my delight and although this was Scotland's only Championship win of the season it couldn't have come at a better time. The Lions squad was still to be picked and I had my heart set on going to New Zealand.

I had one more ordeal to face that night, being told I must make an effort to attend the official dinner with the rest of the team. I got to the Hilton to find the first item on the menu was spinach quiche. I had one look and The Bear took me home to our hotel where I spent the rest of the night either sweating or freezing.

Scotland had another fixture that season, against the Barbarians, to mark the opening of the new Murrayfield East Stand. Personally I regretted that the punters should lose this favourite bit of terracing for it was great to see that sea of faces as you came out of the tunnel and the way they roared you on was something marvellous. But it is a wonderful stand and there's no doubt about that.

Before that match against the Barbarians, however, the Lions squad for New Zealand was to be chosen. I was told that if I were selected I'd probably get a telephone call from one of the Scottish selectors on the Sunday night. I pottered around in the garden, a bag of nerves, and went to bed early. Then came a call about 10.30 p.m. It was a customer inquiring about the price of tyres! Up early next morning, I waited on the postman who of course had to be late that day. I was in the kitchen when Val came through with the letters and sure enough amongst them was one from the SRU. I ripped it open to find it was an invitation to play against the Barbarians on 26 March 1983. I broke down then as I thought I'd missed the boat so far as the Lions were concerned.

I phoned Roy Laidlaw and his wife Joy told me that he'd gone to work but that in any case it would be 11 a.m. before we'd know. That buoyed me up for a wee while and I had the radio on for the 11 a.m. news, as well as Ceefax on TV. Still nothing happened, but I did get a call from one of my Hawick pals saying he'd seen on TV that Peter Wheeler, the English hooker, wasn't going, but Ciaran Fitzgerald, the Irish skipper, was going as the tour captain. He admitted he didn't know if I was in the party.

Then one of the Press boys phoned and his first words were "Congratulations". Talk about relief. Then I looked at Val, who put a brave face on things and congratulated me. I knew deep down, though, she was hating the thought of my going away, especially as she was seven months pregnant by this time.

The Barbarians match was enjoyable although we lost 26-13, maybe because none of the eight Scots selected for the tour party, of which seven played in the fixture, was particularly keen to be injured. One of our lads who was a standby for the tour, Keith Robertson, had the hard luck to get injured after only seven minutes of the match. The giant 18-stone Hennie Bekker tackled and fell on him and Keith had to be whipped into hospital for an operation to a severely dislocated collar bone.

One enjoyable moment before the game was when we were presented to Princess Anne, who had a word with each of the boys. It was wee Roy Laidlaw who made the classic remark, "We'll have to stop meeting like this, Ma'am", which had the spectators wondering why HRH was laughing.

The press up king. There wasn't much else to do.

The month of April was taken up with being kitted out and also getting congratulations and presentations from the various clubs I'd been associated with. Then, on my birthday, 3 May, my mum, dad and brother arrived to drive me to Edinburgh Airport. We had to leave early and I went upstairs to say goodbye to Roddy. He wouldn't get up and he didn't say cheerio . . . I'm sure he sensed I'd be gone for a long time. It was an awful wrench leaving Val and him behind. But she knew I'd worked for this day for the past ten years and no way was she going to stop me now . . . a great girl.

Once we got to London there was a reception at New Zealand House and on 5 May we took off for Auckland via Los Angeles and Tahiti. We soon settled to the routine of training and shortly after our arrival I remember playing a game of golf on a course where the greens were fenced round to keep the sheep off— hardly St Andrews.

Our first game was against Wanganui on 14 May and we won very easily by 47-15. The next night we were in Auckland and Roy was duty boy. We were having dinner when he rushed in to tell me there was a telephone call for me from Scotland. It was my mum and dad to say Val had produced our son, Ross, who weighed in at just under seven pounds. I was sorry to be so far away but delighted naturally about the event and the boys and I had a few beers to celebrate. In fact New Zealand has a special place in my heart ever since I was there in 1983. I'll never forget how the New Zealanders took me and my family to their hearts and every time I look at the toys they gave me to bring back for Ross I think of my friends over there.

I was brought down to earth with a bang next day, though, for I wasn't in the team to play Auckland. It was a hard game and we lost 13-12, which was not the happiest of results considering the tour had not yet properly got under way. The Auckland match was bruising and aggressive, dominated by Gary Whetton and Andy Haden. I was particularly impressed with Whetton. Unfortunately, apart from the defeat Terry Holmes got a nasty cut on the head. I hadn't yet been picked but my chance came at Rotorua on 21 May, against Bay of Plenty. I can't tell you how good it was to pull on the Lions No.2 shirt. To make things even better we won 34-16. In that game against Bay of Plenty there was a big punch-up within the first five minutes. Strangely, it seemed to calm everyone down as though now the preliminaries were out of the way we could get down to playing rugby. Bay of Plenty were led by my opposite number Rikka Reid, a very exciting player who set the crowd alight every time he handled the ball.

Again, I was really touched by the kindness of people at Rotorua. They kept giving me presents for Ross, and the cleaners even left a gift on the pillow of my bed. A picture of Val and Ross had by this time been wired to me.

Over to Wellington where the Lions won 27-19 although Fitzgerald didn't play so well. The Wellington game was another bruising fixture with fireworks from the start. But the Lions forwards gradually got their game together and by winning we put the tour back on the right track, temporarily at least. The weather was good, which may have been the downfall of the New Zealanders because they call it wet and windy Wellington.

Although I didn't play in that match, I was adopted by the local Wellington School where we trained. It's one of those nice tour traditions that a school adopts a player and follows his progress, providing a scrap book at the end of the tour. The player goes along

119

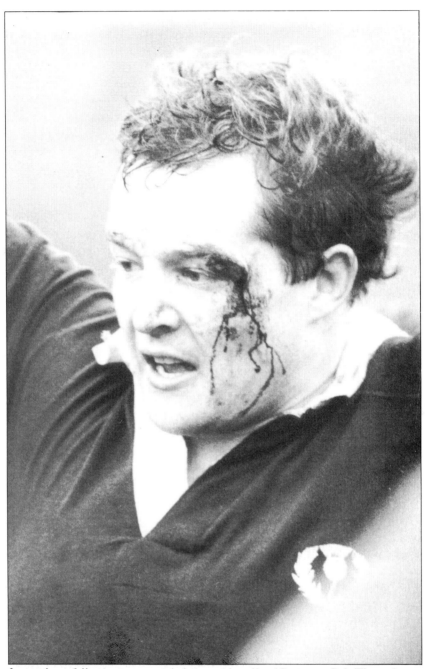

I must have fallen on to someone's boot accidentally. (Courtesy: Bob Thomas)

to see the boys and have talks and altogether it's a very friendly interlude from the tough round of training and games.

I wasn't picked again against Manawatu, our next match, and both Jim Calder and I were beginning to feel pretty bitter. We wanted to know what we had to do to be selected on some kind of semi-permanent basis. I collared the coach, Jim Telfer, and put it to him. He assured me that if I proved I was playing better than Fitzy I'd be picked.

Well, with that assurance straight from the horse's mouth, I was determined to get a Test place for my boys, Roddy and Ross. Next day, in addition to the ordinary team training, Jim and I had extra training and then followed on with more of the same with The Bear.

On the Saturday of the game we found Fitzy practising throwing into the forwards in the car park, things were going so badly in the line-out. And that was to set the pattern for the tour.

The pattern of games in New Zealand was that of an abrasive, intimidating start and again this happened at Manawatu where the home forwards really bullied the Lions pack. However the Lions won that match 25-18.

The final match before the first Test was at Ashburton against Mid-Canterbury. I was relieved to be picked and more relieved when we won 26-6. The Bear was in terrific form, so much so that his opposite number admitted that he hadn't felt so mangled before in his life.

On we went on our travels once more to Christchurch and the big one. Again I was passed over. Jim and I remained determined to prove our fitness and despite torrential rain we set out to do some extra training accompanied by John Beattie. After half a mile John gave up, saying he found we were going too fast for him. Jim and I tried to run each other into the ground and finished up with a sprint to the hotel.

I phoned Val on the Friday night and heard my new son for the first time, bawling his head off. It was a sad blow that I couldn't hold him in my arms and give him a cuddle.

The game itself was one I reckon we should have won. But Fitzgerald kept throwing the ball squint and also lost the tight-head count, so we finished up losing by 16-12.

Next day we were able to relax and we were invited out shooting. My syndicate didn't even see a duck, but it was beautiful countryside and we all enjoyed ourselves. I struck up a great friendship with a wee boy called Andrew Stokes whose dad had a farm.

Our midweek game was against West Coast and I was picked. We won 52-16, then got a ticking off from the chairman's wife for collapsing the scrum. In fact it was West Coast who were doing the damage and we found all teams did this once they felt our controlled scrummage.

I remember Roy Laidlaw was captain that day and when we retired to the bar one of the boys decided to do some button ripping. This involves grabbing a shirt and pulling in opposite directions so the buttons pop off. Wee Roy, who had been celebrating the victory rather heartily, went over to his opposite number who unfortunately was wearing a pullover. Undeterred, Roy tried to turn it into a cardigan. In the end we had to restrain the Kiwi and rescue Roy who was still wondering why the opposing scrum-half was upset.

Our next stop was Invercargill and a victory over Southland by 41-3 with Nigel Melville, who had by now replaced the injured Terry Holmes, making his debut on the tour.

I played my fourth game of the tour against Wairapa Bush at Masterton and we won 57-10 with The Bear again in immense form. Also in the team that day was Steve Boyle, the England lock who had only managed to get into two or at most three games. He was getting a bit of stick from back home. So just to be seen on the TV as playing, Steve put yellow fluorescent tape round his ears and the cuffs of his jersey. And, naturally, in half-an-hour he pulled a hamstring and had to come off the field!

Back to Wellington and the second Test on 18 June. Again I wasn't selected and neither was The Bear who had been playing so magnificently. The game was lost 9-0 and the tour was on a downer. At dinner that night two of the Kiwis admitted they were glad that the pair of us had not been picked and I suppose that was at least a back-handed compliment.

We had a bit of a holiday after that and went fishing with the ex-world champion Marlin fisherman Snooks Fuller. I had the satisfaction of catching the only fish from our boat, a 25 lb yellow tailed Kingfisher.

Our next match was against North Auckland but again I wasn't picked and I was wondering what I had to do to get into a Test side. Certainly I would never be fitter and never play better. There was some more reassurance from Telfer and in the meantime I managed to make a phone call to Val who told me not to tour again. Anyway we won the match 21-12 although Fitzgerald lost three strikes against the head.

On Tuesday 28 June came my big chance . . . or so I thought. I was in the team to play at Christchurch against Canterbury. Unfortunately we didn't have a spot-on goal kicker and Hugo MacNeill missed enough kicks in the first-half to have tied the result up. There were also some dodgy refereeing decisions and we went down by 22-20. It was a frustrating, disappointing result.

The team was announced for the third Test at Dunedin on 2 July just before the previous day's training. I wasn't in it. I felt deflated but glad that at least five of the Scots boys in the party had been included.

I went down to Jim Telfer's room that night. I knew I should have been picked, the Press knew it and most of the boys on the tour came up and said how sorry they were that I hadn't been chosen. I take my hat off to Telfer. He wouldn't say anything against the tour captain or manager . . . both Irish. But I knew myself he would have picked the side on current playing performances and not on past reputations.

The game itself took place in appalling conditions, with helicopters flying over the pitch to try and dry out the ground. It was an exciting encounter and the Scots, particularly John Rutherford who was operating at centre, played especially well. It was however another defeat, by 15-8, and of course that meant there was no hope now of squaring the Test series.

One thing which sticks in my mind after the Dunedin match was that the 30 players taking part were soaked within minutes of going on to the pitch. When they came off I'm sure some of them were suffering from hypothermia. Bottles of rum and brandy were brought into the dressing room but with empty stomachs — the boys only had a light lunch — some started celebrating a little too early. The same was happening in the All Blacks' dressing room although they had something to celebrate being three games up. At the official dinner I soon found out it was safer to be under the table than sitting at it. For if you popped your head up you were liable to be hit by an unidentified flying object . . . usually a roll.

I got a bit of consolation in the next match against Hawkes Bay at Napier when I led the pack. We won 25-19 and I scored my first try for the Lions, but it really wasn't a lot of compensation for being passed over for a Test place. I phoned home again and Roddy told me he'd won his school race. How I wished I had been there to see him!

At home with Roddy and Ross — no longer a baby. (Courtesy: Bob Thomas)

Our next game was against Counties and we won 25-16, with Ollie Campbell kicking a magnificent penalty goal from about ten metres inside his own half. After the match a few of us, as was our wont, went out training. Some of the spectators had stayed behind and gave us abuse. We tried to ignore them until suddenly I found myself flat on my face, hit from behind by one of the yobs. I looked up to see Eddie Butler and Gerry McLoughlin chasing the culprit up through the stand. Fortunately for him they couldn't get their hands on him. I can laugh at it now but it could have been pretty serious.

Next day we travelled on to Hamilton to play Waikato, which was to be my final tour match. I shared a room with Bob Norster of Wales. You get to know all kinds of guys when you're on tour. Some can enter a room and make it look like a rubbish tip in two seconds flat. But Bob was the most immaculate rugby player I've seen on my travels. He couldn't pass a mirror without checking his hair and tie were in place and his suitcase was packed in a way to delight a Guards RSM. On top of being clean and super-tidy he was a smashing bloke and we soon struck up a friendship which still lasts.

I think I played my best rugby of the tour in that match. I scored a try and came within an ace of adding two more. We ran out winners by a convincing 40-13. However for the Test team for the final match at Auckland on 16 July neither I nor The Bear were included. The match itself was a nightmare and our boys were relieved when the final whistle went and we had lost all four Tests, the last by 38-6.

I was now sharing with Roger Baird who had been concussed during the game and I sat up the whole night looking after him and making cups of tea. So I wasn't drowning my sorrows. Before we left New Zealand the next day however we started off with a champagne breakfast to which the Scots boys did justice — the champagne more than the food.

It was a long, tedious flight back to London and all I was looking forward to was seeing Val, Roddy and my new son Ross. When we arrived I phoned Val to let her know my time of landing at Edinburgh. However we managed to get a flight which left a half hour before our scheduled plane. When we arrived the boys let me through first, but there was no sign of Val. Time went on until most of the lads had been collected and were on their way home. That left Roy Laidlaw and myself plus some of the Press photographers. They went off on a hunt of the airport and came back with Val and Roy's wife, Joy, who had been upstairs with the boys watching the planes land and had not realised we were by this time through the baggage claim. It was wonderful to hold wee Ross for the first time and to be with the family again.

Looking back on the tour the plus points were that I had made so many good friends both amongst the Lions and the New Zealanders, and I was super-fit. But there were a lot of minus points as well. The most serious was the fact that the long tour and my absence had obviously taken its toll on Val who had to go through the trauma of a difficult birth while I was at the other end of the earth. And young Roddy was without a dad for three months at a very vulnerable time. Not that Val has ever blamed me for going on the tour. She knew how much it meant to me and I was only sorry I couldn't reward her and Roddy with the knowledge that I'd played in a Test.

But with the tour manager being Irish and the tour captain also Irish and playing the same position as myself the odds were stacked against me from the start. I still think I should have been called in at least by the third Test when there was still a hope of squaring the series and, of course, that goes for The Bear as well. In the seven games in which we played together we combined to take 35 strikes against the head. Now you'll understand why I rate this man as simply the best prop forward in world rugby.

The Irish captain, the Irish manager and the Scottish coach

The best hooker on tour, or so they say.

One of the games I played in with the British Lions, 1983. (Courtesy: Mike Brett).

formed the selection team. So I was 2-1 down before anything had been decided.

My colleagues praised my standard of play, so did the British and New Zealand Press and I honestly thought I was bound to be picked for the Test side. It was only a matter of waiting until my name was called. But that call never came. Telfer never praised me — I didn't expect him to for Jim isn't that kind of guy — but neither did Willie John McBride the manager or Captain Fitzy, who hardly acknowledged my presence.

Telfer was the only one I could speak to as man to man and ask what I had to do to get into the Test side. Jim did admit that he had done his best and from that I gathered he had probably proposed me for the vital third Test but had been out-voted by the Irish mafia.

I can honestly say it's not a question of sour grapes. But I reckon I and a few others should have at least been given the chance to try and drag the tour out of the mud when a win was vital. It was not to be however and that elusive Test call never came.

To add to my suffering, throughout the tour whenever Ciaran was playing I had the ritual of watching him trying to brush up on his throwing in the car park. It was frustrating for me to see, for he just couldn't throw the ball straight let alone find his jumpers. Maybe I should have tried to help him but I was gunning for his place.

I also thought that throughout the tour Ciaran Fitzgerald as skipper adopted all the wrong tactics. I don't mean only on the field where a man in that position is expected to set an example. But, perhaps even more importantly on such trips, off-field.

I know there must have been a lot of pressure on Fitzy but he could have tried to share his problems with the rest of the squad. Instead the only bloke I saw him really talking with was a supporter who was

If it wasna for your wellies.
L-R: Andrew Stokes (Little boy), Roger Baird, Michael Keirnan, C. Deans.
(Courtesy: Bob Thomas)

Now do you believe a man can fly? Lions v Waikato '83 tour to New Zealand.

following the tour. Seldom would he join the boys at all, even for a sing-song, and he was in the habit of taking solitary walks. As an Army officer, he seemed to take the view that he was the Captain with a capital C and we were just the privates. You might win wars that way but not tours.

Chapter 12

GRAND SLAM

ONE positive thing at least had come out of the tour of New Zealand. Until then the Scotland players had lacked confidence in their own ability. We were often in awe at the feats accomplished by players of other countries. But having trained, played and shared the joys and disappointments of some of those fabulous rugby legends among the British Lions we Scots laddies realised that often their breaking point wasn't nearly as good as ours. When things went wrong they were too often ready to chuck it. The confidence we picked up was shared amongst the rest of the squad when we got into training for what was to be a glory season.

As one of the breed I can confirm that the Scots are probably the most thrawn race in the world. It is not enough for this wee country to produce a champion jockey like Willie Carson . . . he must be injured or suspended or preferably both before the championship counts. I am convinced that the only reason Bonnie Prince Charlie didn't go all the way to London after reaching Derby was that the clan chiefs found it all too easy. They decided to give the English a sporting chance by yomping back to prepare for Culloden.

There may lie the reason why Scots rugby men took from 1938 to 1984 to win the Triple Crown and from 1925 to the same year to win the Grand Slam. They could have done it earlier, but so often it looked so easy they seemed to do everything to throw their chances away! Selections often appeared devised to give comfort to the enemy, with guys struggling to stay in the 2nd XV elevated to greater glory than they had ever dreamed about. And there was a tendency also to pick the odd player who was unfit.

Now the selection process is much more intense and in the best possible way professional. Medical men can say whether a man is really fit without going over the border of the jealously guarded privilege of the chosen man being allowed to call off on his own initiative. No player today would risk letting his country and his mates down by going on the field knowing he might break down. Similarly, with the squad session in operation no longer do players just meet up the day before the match, introduce themselves and go out on the field with "do your best" ringing in their ears.

As the 1983/84 season got under way it was obvious that Jim Telfer, unfairly blamed for the New Zealand British Lions defeats, was determined to show what a good coach he really was. The selection convener was Ian McGregor who, like Telfer, had played in the pack for Scotland. He was tired of making post-match statements limited to pointing out that Scotland did not have the resources of other countries as he tried to explain away the latest defeat.

Prop Jim Aitken was to be captain that season. The oldest man in the side, he was nicknamed Big Daddy. Like Telfer he had suffered disappointment. No call had come for him from the injury-hit Lions although he had remained in training.

So, with a disillusioned coach, a disappointed skipper and a selection boss desperate to change excuses for Scotland into triumphant speeches, things looked so bad that for once we might win the lot. The bookies certainly didn't take that view, however. England were the great hopes of the pre-season so far as the Triple Crown went, while France as usual were favourites to take the Grand Slam.

Our build-up was like the curate's egg, both good and bad. The Scotland B team won against their Irish opposite numbers at Melrose, but the Scottish trial ended in a win for the Possibles versus the Probables. We did have one big morale booster when drawing 25-25 with the All Blacks at Murrayfield in November, in a game marred by some bad sportsmanship. In the dying seconds Brian Anderson, the international referee, signalled to French referee Rene

Beating England at Murrayfield on our way to the Grand Slam.

Hourquet that, from his position as linesman, he had seen a punch thrown at Jim Pollock as the Blacks went for the winning score. The New Zealand manager Bryce Rope complained afterwards that touch judges were spoiling the game of rugby. To that Telfer replied that in his three months in New Zealand with the Lions he had never complained once about touch judge or refereeing decisions.

Still, the team went down to Cardiff in January 1984 heartened by that draw and attempting to bring off a second successive win at the National Stadium.

There was never the slightest doubt that the Welsh were going to be mighty hard to beat. Both their coach John Bevan and their captain Eddie Butler were under threat of the chop, following a shock earlier defeat by Romania. I don't think the Welsh ever really approved of Butler as skipper. I thought him a nice guy and a good player. But the fact that he could speak French and taught at a posh educational establishment didn't go down so well with fans more used to the rugged personalities of miners and steelmen.

There was a lot of snow around in Scotland so we had to give up any idea of training on the back pitch at Murrayfield and instead had a session on the banks of the Firth of Forth. It was good to sense the relaxed, confident air about the side but we certainly couldn't afford

In singing voice on our way to our victorious Triple Crown dinner in Ireland 1984.

to relax once we travelled to Wales and stepped on to the Cardiff pitch.

Wales, knowing that referee Owen Doyle was handling his first game at the highest level, ran at us in the torrid early moments like demented dragons, not even attempting to play by the rules. But our rucking, always the main plank in Telfer's strategy, was first-rate that day and we eventually took the steam out of the Welsh pack.

Then David Leslie, operating at the tail of the line-out, and myself struck up a great rapport. I would throw the ball over the heads of the Welsh forwards and there would be Leslie grabbing it and setting up the initial attacks. At full-back too Peter Dods was as sound as the Rock of Gibraltar. At the end of the day we won 15-9 and Dods had got seven points from two conversions and a penalty goal. The experience gained on the Lions tour by Iain Paxton helped him score a try, while our Big Daddy Aitken, helped by a shove from Leslie, got his first try for Scotland.

In the short time between the final whistle and the official dinner the wine suppliers had managed to get on the labels the winning score. Aitken was not impressed. "They knew they were going to be beat and just guessed the score."

The streets of Cardiff were strangely quiet that night. The Welsh chorus had been silenced and Scotland were on the march.

Probably the worst thing that happened to England before the start of the Five Nations championship was the fact that they had beaten New Zealand. It gave them an inflated notion of their real strength. More importantly it stifled any thoughts of planning a more expansive type of game.

Apart from the fact that this was the 100th match with the Calcutta Cup at stake there was another personal reason why Scotland wanted to do well against the Auld Enemy at Murrayfield. England captain Bill Beaumont had been quoted as saying some of the Scots were over the hill and particularly lock Bill Cuthbertson. Now Cuthbertson is what the Irish call 'a lovely man'. He's also a sentimental man. And the remark hurt him deeply. Remember we Scots are tribal people — insult one and you insult the lot. So we went on to the pitch in particularly determined mood.

England, under hooker Peter Wheeler, were keen to capitalise on the strength of their forwards and the boot of full-back Dusty Hare. But Telfer had marked Hare down for special attention and John Rutherford was a key figure in the strategy. Rutherford was immense that day. He kicked awkward hanging balls which arrived at the same time as speedy Roger Baird on the England full-back. The result was that Dusty missed six out of eight goal attempts and the two penalties he did kick were the sum total of England's score.

Both our centres, David Johnston and Euan Kennedy, touched down tries. Unfortunately both Kennedy and Cuthbertson were hurt in the match and were ruled out of the rest of the championship. But the value of the squad system was shown in that against England both John Beattie and Jim Pollock slotted in and we took the Cup with a score of 18-6.

It was all going so well for Scotland now — a draw with the All Blacks, two international wins and the B team on top of their victory over Ireland had beaten France B in Albi. Maybe it was looking so good that we might blow it yet again.

So off we went to Dublin with the Triple Crown the glittering prize and Telfer grimly determined to make sure we took it. Because of security precautions we drove through the gloaming to our hotel well outside Dublin in a coach without lights and with a three-man police motorcycle escort. My own view is that if anyone is going to be safe in Ireland it's someone playing sport, for the Irish themselves forget any bitter differences when picking their rugby teams, which contain

The Edinburgh Lord Provost congratulates us after our Triple Crown victory over Ireland. We had had a heavy night.

Dead-eyed Dods. Even with this keeker we beat France, Grand Slam victory 1984.

a mixture of North and South players. Nevertheless, the security was always there and served to heighten the tension before what was already a vital match.

Our Friday morning training session at a nearby ground was an object lesson for any psychology student. We had brought in Alister Campbell, a team-mate of mine, for his first cap to replace the injured Cuthbertson. Telfer told me to keep throwing the ball towards Campbell. "Now Alister, come in for the next ball," he'd say time after time in the middle of a hailstorm which sent the spectators scuttling for the warmth of the clubhouse bar. Then he'd add to the rest of the forwards, "See the way Alister is jumping for the ball — I want the rest of you to do the same." It was good thinking and it worked, for next day Alister played more like a veteran than a rookie.

Ireland, whose Old Guard had confounded everyone for so long were obviously going through a bad patch. But at stand-off they had Tony Ward who on his day is worth two ordinary players.

Grand Slam celebrations: giz a drink o that! (Courtesy: Bob Thomas)

Our star that day however was Roy Laidlaw, who scored two tries at about the same spot. Unfortunately Roy got a bang on the head and had to be replaced by Gordon Hunter who fitted in nicely. We knew we had the Irish beaten early on and ran out winners by a massive 32-9 total. Hunter, indicentally, was in the wars after the game. Running off the pitch he collided with an excited schoolboy spectator and had his cheekbone fractured. So we had paid a price for the first Triple Crown since 1938.

Fortunately Laidlaw wasn't as badly hurt as we had feared and he was able to make the journey back to Edinburgh with the team on the Sunday. When some of the boys asked him how his head felt the Jed man replied, "No' half as sair as yours . . . I wasn't out drinking last night."

One of the funniest incidents following the game was provided by a certain member of the team. Because our hotel was about 20 miles away from the city centre the SRU had agreed we could share taxis and charge them up when returning from the official dinner. The coach was about to start next morning and some kind soul had packed his missing team-mate's suitcase for him. Suddenly the player in question, still in evening dress, rolled up. "Who," he asked, "will pay this cabbie?" Without flickering an eyelid Ian McGregor, the selection convener, said, "You will, son. It'll teach you to come home earlier."

Ach well, you don't really expect to be a hero just for helping gain a Crown . . . if you play for Scotland. At any rate we got home to a wonderful welcome at the airport and the Lord Provost hustled up some champagne.

But we still had the toughest task to accomplish . . . to beat France at Murrayfield and take the Grand Slam. Both sides were unbeaten and a titanic struggle was on the cards.

We were helped by the fact that Roy was passed fit to play following that head knock in Ireland, and by the usual meticulous preparation of the side by Telfer. When we trained we wore white jerseys instead of blue. This was because, due to the usual courtesies, the French would retain their blue shirts and Jim didn't want any of us in a moment of forgetfulness passing out to one of them.

The day of the match coincided by chance with Telfer's 44th birthday. He had enough cakes donated to him by everyone from fans to photographers to give him tummy ache for a year. But Jim is not the kind of guy to count his chickens before they hatch or eat his cake without knowing he had something to celebrate.

So the vital day, 17 March 1984, dawned.

It was the biggest game of our careers, Telfer told us. The match was a complete sell-out and you couldn't get a ticket for a gold-mine. Stomachs were churning long before the bus arrived at the Braids Hotel and I was glad when we eventually got away. A quick rendering of *Flower of Scotland* before we got off, then through the hail of good wishes and slaps on the back.

What a roar went up when we inspected the pitch. It was like the lid being blown off a pan of tatties. Back to the dressing room, strapping put on, muscles loosened up and a talk from Adam Robson, the then President, and out on to the field.

The French looked really mean and menacing. Rives was moving up and down like a lion stalking a deer. The referee's whistle went and the French kicked off. It was soon evident they had come to win. They powered into every scrum, maul and line-out.

One thing we had learned during the campaign was to defend and tackle and we needed all our determination to halt Rives' men. The French missed an early opportunity to score but eventually Jerome Gallion broke from a scrum and got a try which Jean-Patrick Lescarboura converted.

But all was not lost. It had taken a mighty effort by the French to get that score and they must have wondered what they needed to do

We've really done it. A dream come true.

to crack our defence wide open. Our full-back Peter Dods got a penalty goal to make it 6-3 in favour of the French at the interval.

It was midway through the second-half and after Lescarboura had kicked a penalty goal that the turning point came for Scotland. From a French throw-in to a two-man line-out the ball was intended for Gallion, the play maker. Instead David Leslie was there for Scotland and in the collision which followed Gallion was stretchered off.

The Bear was simply immense that day. He really destroyed the French scrum. Their second row were punching him all through the game and his face was badly marked afterwards, but The Bear just growled, absorbed it all and put on more pressure.

I next felt we had it won when there was a scrum in the middle of the field. When it broke up the French forwards were bickering amongst themselves and that was a sure sign that they were rattled.

Sure enough French indiscipline did cost them dear and Dods, in magnificent kicking form, put over two penalty goals. France, though, were by no means finished and Lescarboura had a good drop goal. Again Dods kicked a penalty to level the scores.

Then at 4.23 p.m. that afternoon came the most exciting try I've seen scored during my career. We had worked our way up to the French line and when I threw in the idea was that we would peel from the line-out. However Jean-Luc Joinel got his fingertips to the ball and deflected it towards the French line. Jim Calder reached up, grabbed it and fell over the line for a try which Dods converted. French frustration then saw Serge Blanco hurling himself at Dods in the closing minutes and the Scottish full-back kicked the resulting penalty just to make sure.

Peter Dods got a black eye during the game which had anxious mums shielding their children from the sight. But he played magnificently and scored 17 points in our 21-12 victory. Dods finished up with a new championship record for Scotland, having notched 50 points in one international season. Scotland finished up with the elusive Grand Slam and for once Telfer finished up with a smile.

Captain of the Grand Slam team was Jim Aitken, the Gala prop. Now it's certainly a great honour to captain Scotland at any time but particularly when they win the Slam. But I reckon Aitken was lucky. He was given a team which was exactly the right blend and would have won for anyone.

Always an aggressive player, it's no secret that Jim wasn't exactly loved by any of the Hawick team in his early days when big Norman Pender used to grind him down. However as Jim is in the grain trade and Norman keeps pigeons they eventually became buddies, with Aitken supplying some feed for the birds!

I don't think Jim was an outstanding prop. He made a lot of correct decisions, he prodded and shouted at people, though I'm afraid he never motivated me. But he was in the right place at the right time. He was made captain before the Grand Slam year when we went down to Twickenham as no-hopers and came back with a win. However to my mind the real credit for the Grand Slam goes to the boys who were on the Lions tour and knew more than anyone else about the opposition. At any rate, after the Grand Slam I feel Jim should have retired instead of waiting to be dropped. That was a sad ending when he could have got out at the top.

For my part, I felt so proud to be part of history. We had done the impossible to the delight of every Scot in the world. And what a day for Jim Telfer who had swallowed all the criticism in New Zealand where we had the Test whitewash. He had answered his critics through the actions of his team on the field.

The dressing room was awash with champagne bottles. There must have been about 60 people milling about, all hugging each

Receiving our Grand Slam video from the Beeb. L-R: Alasdair Milne, J. Aitken, C. Deans. (Courtesy: Ian Southern)

other as if they'd never met for years. Then a bath, shave and out to the bus for the official dinner where the celebrations continued as you can imagine.

I don't think any of the boys heard the speeches.

Next morning at breakfast I kept being tannoyed to take a phone call at reception and each time I went up there was no call for me. But I spotted John Rutherford giggling away after the third time I'd been summoned and I found he had taken the microphone from the band in the early hours and was having me on.

After breakfast it was time to get down the road to Peebles where I had promised to start a charity race. And when I got home it was sleeves up as I became labourer to the brickie who was building an extension to my house. There's no peace for the wicked or rugby players!

Function followed function to celebrate the Slam win, ranging from a reception in Edinburgh Castle hosted by George Younger, then Secretary of State for Scotland, to one by the Lord Provost of Edinburgh, another by Lothian Regional Council and a further one by the BBC. It was as hectic as playing.

I was now looking forward, as were many of the boys, to a nice peaceful summer. Some of us had been playing rugby almost non-stop since 1981. But I had two further engagements that season. One was to take part at Mansfield Park in a charity match for cancer relief which had been organised by a local bobby. I was proud to see that all the Grand Slam party turned out to help.

I don't swear that it's true but the story went round that Jim Aitken, a Gala fanatic, was asked what had given him the most pleasure during the season — winning the Triple Crown or the Grand Slam. To which Jim is alleged to have replied that putting on a green Hawick jersey topped the lot!

My last game of the period was when I went to Cardiff to play for a Welsh Union President's XV against Wales to mark the opening of a new stand at the Arms Park.

I pulled out of the Romanian tour party for May as did Iain Milne and Iain Paxton. Earlier Hawick had won the Scottish and Border championship titles, so I felt justified in taking it easy for a while.

Chapter 13

SALESMAN TO HER MAJESTY

THERE was an unexpected thrill that summer when the Grand Slam party were invited with their wives to the Queen's Garden Party at Holyrood. We all met for lunch first. To my horror I found all the rest of the lads were in grey morning suits while I was in black. Val was not at all amused. Imagine my satisfaction, then, to find that once we got to the Palace everyone else was in black and the rest of the boys stood out like sore thumbs.

While we were there Jim Telfer came over to tell us the Duke of Buccleuch wanted to see us. He in turn said the Queen wished to meet the squad and we were escorted to the passageway on the lawn where Her Majesty stopped to speak to various individuals.

During the course of her conversation with me she remarked that it must be great fun to do nothing but play rugby. I pointed out we all had full-time jobs and she asked me what I did. I told her I was in the double glazing business and asked if she was in the market for windows for Holyroodhouse. My joke brought a smile but no order. But I can say that I'm the only double glazing man to have tried to sell windows to the Queen!

It was a big thrill for everyone of course and especially the wives. The one sour note was when she asked Keith Robertson what he did and he replied that he was one of the three million as he was out of

143

Selling windows to The Queen — a real treat for Val.

work at the time. I don't think H.M. was particularly amused to be reminded of the country's economic problems at a social gathering like that.

At the start of the 1984/85 season I received an invitation to take part in a RFU President's XV to play an England XV at Twickenham to mark the 75th anniversary of the opening of the ground. The President's XV was composed of players from all over the world, with the exception of Australia who had a major tour on

144

Looking through the window.

their hands shortly after the game. We soon settled together and although Andy Irvine had to drop out as captain because of injury, another Scot, David Leslie, took over. I think everyone enjoyed the game and particularly the result — a 27-10 win over the England side.

YOU'RE A HOOKER, THEN

Then, before really getting down to serious business, I took part in the BBC series *Superstars*. The contest was held at RAF Cosford. Imagine my feelings when I found most of the guys I was competing against had just returned from the Olympic games and were super-fit. Not only that, they'd been training specially for the *Superstars* crown whereas I'd just come into the competition for fun.

One of the competitors who really shook me was Neil Adams, the judo expert. He started doing press-ups from the handstand position. When I saw that I shook my head at Val and realised this was no place for an amateur rugby player. However I soldiered on and despite being cuffed I enjoyed the experience.

In the cycling event I was competing against Joe Lydon of rugby league fame. He was a great guy but we got into an awful fankle after carrying our bicycles over a gate. As we sped off, our handlebars entwined and he went crashing down one way and I the other. All we could do was laugh it off.

I entered for the swimming event as I'd heard no one else was going in for that . . . but because I was the sole competitor, I wasn't given any points! My bad luck followed me when I got to the final of the canoeing competition . . . and fell out of the canoe. I also managed to fall out of my blocks at the sprint event.

I rather fancied myself in the 800 metres and after 400 was only four seconds outside Seb Coe's world record. But I tied up before the end of the race. Well, you can't win them all. It would have been nice, though, to have won even a single event against fellows like Adams, Lydon, Robin Brew, Steve Otley, Andrew Redgrave and Phil Brown. However I admit I was well outclassed and it was good to get back to rugby.

On 1 December 1984 South took on the touring Australians at Mansfield Park and I was made captain. We Border boys had something to prove, for the previous October the All Blacks had thrashed us by 30-9. This time we were on song against the Aussies in a stamina-testing match and, with Peter Dods kicking the winning points in the dying minutes, we ran out 9-6 winners.

The Aussies, by the way, had been complaining about wanting to do something different during their short stay in the Borders, before the game. With the co-operation of a few worthies they were taken out at night to poach some salmon and thoroughly enjoyed the experience. The only snag was that on the second night they were nearly caught and had to leave their catch in the woods.

This is how the Aussies end up — a 9-6 win to South.

The Australians left the Borders to play Glasgow on 4 December and while the lads from the west side of the country put up a fine show it was the tourists who triumphed by 26-12. But at least we in the South had the honour of having inflicted the only Saturday defeat the tourists sustained on their triumphant march across Britain.

There was no doubt that their coach, Alan Jones, who is probably the most erudite man ever in that position — he used to be a speech writer for the Australian Prime Minister — had only one thing on his mind. That was to lead the first Aussie team to take the Grand Slam over here . . . and Scotland were the last stumbling block to that ambition.

After the South win I had been hoping I might have the honour of leading Scotland in the match which took place at Murrayfield on 8 December. However the selectors went for Roy as captain and brought in four new caps, including two Border forwards — Gregor Mackenzie and John Jeffrey. Mackenzie's selection was a surprise for it meant Jim Aitken being out of the side. We also had a new coach now with Colin Telfer taking over from Grand Slam Jim Telfer who is no relation. Derrick Grant came into the reckoning as the assistant to Colin.

The game itself was a bit of a disaster for Scotland. The Australians introduced a new dimension to rugby as it had been known up until now in the British Isles . . . that was to concentrate on athleticism amongst the forwards. It was a lesson to us and one which eventually was to help Scotland a lot, for Grant tucked that knowledge away in his wise head and has taught the later Scottish sides that running is not just an art to be mastered by backs.

Mind you, these Australians were excellent in every aspect of the game and their scrummaging was so intense that I hurt my ribs before the end. All our points came from Peter Dods, who kicked four penalty goals, but we never got near to scoring a try. No disgrace however. As Robin Charters said later, "In the closing 15 minutes I think we'd have scored tries against any other country."

So we had met the best and could only hope that none of the Five Nations countries could emulate the Australians. Trying to console the Scots, Jones, the master of the one-liners, said of our decline from Grand Slam greatness, "One day you're the rooster, the next a feather duster." That sums up this funny old game of ours pretty well.

There was consolation for me after that match for I was invited to captain the Barbarians against the Australians in the tourists' final game at Cardiff on 15 December. Unfortunately I had to pass up the honour as my rib injury ruled me out. The Australians finished their wonderful tour with a 37-30 win over the Baa-baas. It was a measure of their success in sticking to running rugby that they scored 400 points in 13 wins, one draw and four defeats.

With the still-celebrating Australians on their way home it was down to hard work in preparation for the Five Nations tournament and the hope that we could bring off another Triple Crown, if not the Slam again.

Such dreams were dashed however in the first match of the campaign when Ireland were visitors to Murrayfield on 2 February 1985. We were beaten for line-out ball and the Irish backs ran everything and ran it well. Once again Peter Dods proved his value

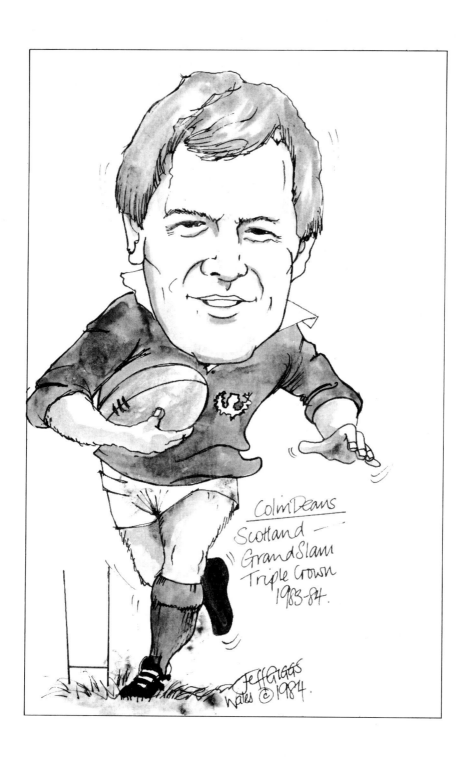

Colin Deans
Scotland —
Grand Slam
Triple Crown
1983-84.

Jeff Giggs
Wales © 1984.

to the side with his deadly accurate kicking, getting four penalty goals, while John Rutherford added one of his famous drop goals. But the Irish deservedly won by 18-15 and it was back to the drawing board for us.

We went to Paris under a new captain in David Leslie. But I don't think anyone could have stemmed the French in the form they displayed. It was obvious they were seeking revenge for what had happened to them at Murrayfield the previous season and they simply ran us ragged. The eventual score was 11-3 to the home team but really it would have been more but for some good defensive work.

One thing both the French and Scots kickers agreed on was that the ball used in the game wasn't suitable. Even Dods managed only one successful penalty goal from three attempts and it was the Frenchman Jean Lescarboura who protested first. He said, and Peter agreed with him, that the ball was far too light.

The trouble was that the French Rugby Union had just signed a new sponsorship deal and agreed to use this particular type of ball. Well, I can understand money is needed to run international rugby but unless the players get the kind of equipment they need there doesn't seem much point.

Wales were the next team we met, at Murrayfield, and again while there was an improvement in the Scots play, we weren't good enough and went down by 25-21. The highlight from our point of view was that Iain Paxton scored a couple of tries from a ploy we had been working on for some time.

There was drama after the match as well when the Welsh coach John Bevan launched a savage attack on the French referee René Hourquet. He said his display had been "diabolical, incompetent" and that "he didn't know what was going on". Poor Hourquet, who doesn't speak English, was obviously upset by the remarks and our skipper Leslie took the opportunity at the official dinner to say, "It's a tradition in rugby that you don't criticise the referee." Like all French refs I think Hourquet was trying to let the game flow and he was certainly as fair to one side as the other. The whole incident left a nasty taste but Hourquet to his credit declined to lodge any official complaint.

England at Twickenham provided us with the last hope of salvaging something from a season which had seen us go from Grand Slam champions to contenders for the wooden spoon. But if you look at the official team picture taken on the famous turf there you'll see a bunch of lads looking for all the world as if the firing squad was waiting to knock them off. So it proved. From the glory of top dogs we'd lost away to Romania, been taken apart by the brilliant Australians and beaten by Ireland, France and Wales. Now came the final humiliation.

Mind you, right up to the final whistle it looked like we could snatch the winning score. But I still have nightmares when I recall seeing Roger Baird, Keith Robertson and John Rutherford in the third minute of injury time, with the ball at their feet, the line at their mercy and not an Englishman within 20 metres of them. A cruel bounce of the ball sent it back between their legs and John actually had to turn to grab it. He got a pass out to Iain Paxton but by this time England had re-grouped and were ready. Rory Underwood stole the ball to deny the score and break every Scots spectator's heart.

About the only thing I can smile about during that weekend was being at the dinner at the Hilton Hotel when my team-mate Alister Campbell was seated at a table full of officials. Whereas normally you have one or two players mixed with the hierarchy, Alister was on his own. One of the English officials, trying to be friendly, turned during the soup course and said, "Alister, don't you think this soup is rather tepid?" "Oh," said Alister, "I thought it was chicken."

But one laugh wasn't enough to erase the bitter memory of that particular season. Of course, as Grand Slam champions we were there to be shot at by everyone else . . . and they didn't spare the ammunition. We also had to contend with a number of injuries and never had a scrap of luck. I know you play for your fate, but now and again you expect a wee bit help from Lady Luck . . . a doubtful decision that goes your way, an interception or a misdemeanour the referee doesn't spot. So far as Scotland was concerned that season our particular Lady Luck had her eyes firmly closed.

So far as my own personal contribution was concerned, I quite frankly felt after that rib injury against the Australians, that I wasn't 100 per cent as fit as normal for the start of the Five Nations tournament. But there it was. People who had been hailing us as heroes the previous season were making the fortunes of the wooden spoon manufacturers and, looking ahead, one wondered what could be done to get us back on song once more.

A five-match tour to North America in May was the first step towards trying to build some kind of revival. I had to decline the invitation to tour because of business commitments however. I had only been a year in my job and most of the winter months had been spent playing rugby. A lot of other experienced players, including Roger Baird, John Rutherford, Keith Robertson and Gerry McGuinness, couldn't make the trip either.

Scotland's run of bad luck continued before the party even set off. Bob Munro, who was our World Cup manager, had been chosen in the same capacity for the North American tour but was struck down with a heart attack. Fortunately he has since made a great recovery. Injuries and unavailability continued to dog the selection committee's plans, with Bob Hogarth, the Kelso scrum-half, calling off, and then Gordon Hunter, another scrum-half, being injured and pulling out.

It was about this time that the idea of a World Cup became known though it didn't particularly excite the Scottish rugby boys who were more intent in getting together a team for the next season which would be capable of wiping out our whitewash disaster.

I was cheered up quite a bit by being selected to play for and lead the Barbarians against Italy in Rome in May 1985. What a trip that was. On the Friday night we got to the Rome Hilton Hotel and some of the boys opted for a night cap. We made our way up to the roof garden bar and had a few lagers.

Next morning at breakfast Mickey Steele-Bodger, who was the tour manager, and who had said we could charge our bills to the Baa-baas, summoned me to his table and gave me one hell of a dressing down. Not because of the amount we had drunk, which was very little, but because they were charging the equivalent of £9 a pint. From then on that particular bar was out of bounds. Mind you, I began to understand the prices when I translated the tariff rates in my room. It worked out at £145 a night for the room alone . . . not the kind of prices you pay in Hawick.

We did the usual tourist things and visited the Sistine Chapel. We were to have had an audience with the Pope. Unfortunately he was having some kind of meeting with his cardinals so we didn't see him. However we did see the Fountain of Trevi and dutifully threw in a few coins. Later we had a magnificent meal at a vineyard near Rome.

Next day we met the Italians. I had to come off near the end with an ankle injury but by then the game was all sewn up and we had won quite comfortably. I remember being very impressed by the England winger Rory Underwood who scored a couple of tries that day.

At least I had salvaged something from the season, having led the South to a win over the Australians and now the Barbarians to victory over Italy.

Chapter 14

CAPTAIN OF SCOTLAND

SEASON 1985/86 started early for me. Again I was given the honour of leading the Barbarians, this time against London Welsh who were celebrating their centenary. The Welsh had been on tour and were extremely fit, so I reckon the Baa-baas did pretty well to beat them that September, even by a fairly narrow margin. Our team on the day included Peter Dods and The Bear, with Mike Kiernan and Willie Anderson of Ireland, Jean Orso of France, Kevin Simms and Rory Underwood of England and Ikey Stephens and Robert Norster of Wales. With players of that calibre around you, you just couldn't help playing well.

During the summer it had been announced that Colin Telfer was packing in as Scotland coach because of business commitments. So my old friend — and often tormentor — Derrick Grant took over, with Ian McGeechan as his assistant. Ian, the loyal little Scot with a Yorkshire accent — he was born in England but his dad was a Scottish soldier — was a player I'd always admired. He and Derrick are on the same wavelength and both are eager to see Scotland play an expanding game. In addition, the Grand Slam coach Jim Telfer returned to be a selector. So it was obvious that the top brass was well aware of the need to get everyone motivated after the disappointments of the previous season.

Matt Duncan: out of may way, Rory!

One of the ways in which we tried to speed up our play was to concentrate on channel one ball. That meant when I hooked the ball went straight back to the scrum-half and it was up to him to get it away immediately. For a comparatively light pack such as we field this is good sense. If you hold the ball in the back row it allows the enemy to set up a defensive system once you do break.

The great benefit, I think, about our way — or rather McGeechan's way — of doing things is that if the ball is transferred quickly enough it lets Gavin Hastings at full-back burst into the line at speed. He's a big lad is Gavin and he's also a guy who likes to use his wingers. There we're lucky to have fellows like Roger Baird, Matt Duncan and Iwan Tukalo to call on. Probably McGeechan has been

155

lucky too, in that he has had the type of personnel who can do the things he wants to see carried out. He and Derrick, to my mind, are the thinking man's coaches.

For myself and the rest of the Scotland hopefuls it was down to work and the fierce competition of the trial at Murrayfield early in January 1986. I was picked as captain of the Blues, or senior side, and I knew that a good win could see me installed as captain of Scotland.

To my dismay I couldn't seem to drum up the commitment I wanted from the boys and the rookie Reds gave us a torrid time, with guys like Gavin and Scott Hastings and Finlay Calder making their mark on the fixture. In addition the Reds were captained by Gary Callander, the Kelso hooker, and I could see my dreams of being the Scots captain vanishing in favour of Gary.

So it was an anxious time for me until the phone rang about 10.40 p.m. on the Tuesday night and I heard Robin Charters' voice telling me that I was to be captain of my country. He read out my team and I came off the phone still in a bit of a daze. I thought back on all the various stages I'd gone through, from playing for Hawick to this final supreme honour. It had been hard going for much of the time. But to run out on the Murrayfield pitch for even one international with that thistle on your jersey makes it all worth while.

When I got the news of my captaincy Val and I were living in a little flat, for we'd sold our house and were waiting to get into our new abode. But we had a wee celebration — just the two of us — and I don't know who was the more pleased. I contacted the rest of the family to let them know the good news. From then on telegrams and good luck cards came flooding in and of course telephone calls from the media boys.

It was a new-look Scottish side I'd been put in charge of, with no fewer than six first caps — Finlay Calder, David Sole and Jeremy Campbell-Lamerton were amongst the forwards, while the Hastings brothers, Gavin and Scott, and Matt Duncan were in the backs.

Our first opponents were the French who came over to Murrayfield. That suited us for the French don't normally travel well and if you get them first on your home ground it's always a great advantage. Against that theory, of course, was the fact that they were fielding practically the same side as had wiped the floor with us the previous season and the additional factor that our side was pretty well experimental. However I was heartened by the air of self-

156

Finlay Calder. (Courtesy: Bob Thomas)

confidence in the Scots camp and the way we knitted together during the hard Thursday training session.

Mind you, I was still as nervous as a cat on a hot tin roof. I remember walking into the tea room at our hotel that night to watch a video when young Scott Hastings piped up, "I say, Dino, could you get me a cup of hot chocolate and some sandwiches before you sit down?" I didn't know whether to laugh or belt him across the ear hole. Here was I, a mature player going out for his 40th cap on the Saturday, and this laddie who hadn't played at all for Scotland was ordering me around like a waiter. But that was typical of Scott and his brother Gavin. They enjoy their Saturday afternoon sport whether they are playing for Watsonians or Scotland. They've got a marvellous outlook and absolutely no nerves.

On the Friday night we went to the cinema to relax and the manager was kind enough to announce at the interval that the Scottish team was present and to ask the audience to wish them well. It was a nice gesture and everyone applauded. It was only spoiled by one punter in front of me who turned round and said eagerly, "Which yin of youse is Kenny Dalglish?" Well, there's no accounting for taste.

Came the day of the game. We had the usual 11 a.m. meeting of the team, followed by a light lunch, then on to Murrayfield. When we ran out on to the field for the match I felt about ten feet tall, having the honour of leading Scotland for the first time. We had won the toss and I elected to kick off.

What a disaster that nearly turned out to be. Gavin Hastings kicked off. The ball went straight into touch and we all thought the French would want us to take the kick again or scrum at the half-way line. Not a bit of it. Before we had collected our thoughts and trundled back, scrum-half Pierre Berbizier had thrown the ball to Daniel Dubroca, the French skipper, got the return pass and scored a spectactular try . . . all within the space of 19 seconds!

What a blow. As skipper for the first time all I could do was to encourage the lads to get going again. And, give them their due, every man obliged.

We were still trailing 12-7 at the interval. But thankfully all of the new caps were doing better than anyone had a right to expect and Gavin Hastings had his kicking boots on. Playing his first game for Scotland, prop David Sole showed what a tremendous prospect he is, while Finlay Calder whom I'd always rated very highly was magnificent and Matt Duncan snuffed out attempts by the French winger Patrick Esteve to score tries. Put simply, the mix was right — the selectors had chosen the right team — and when we came off with a win of 18-17 my heart went out to the players and selectors.

The French, as so often in the past, helped to defeat themselves. They tried to browbeat our team, knowing there were six new boys involved. But time after time Dave Burnett, the Irish referee, penalised them for their excesses and Gavin scored all our points with six magnificent penalty goals.

When we trooped off the field I was full of pride for having been allowed to lead a Scottish team like this. There were no superstars in the side. No cliques. We just trusted each other and we thought on the same wavelength, so much so that before the match started we were in a huddle singing *Flower of Scotland*, which I reckon is the tune to bring a lump to the throat and a tear to the eye of every loyal Scot.

The dinner which followed was a champagne affair, but I opted out of anything too heavy as I had been invited to take part in the *Question of Sport* programme and was due to go down to Manchester with Val on the Sunday. I was rather taken aback to find that one of my opponents in the televised quiz programme was Rob Andrew, who proceeded to tell me how good England were and what they would do to Scotland. I thought perhaps he'd never read the reports of the Murrayfield match or seen the television broadcast so I forgave him. Later Val was telling me that his girlfriend of the time confessed to her that she had to make an appointment to see Rob because of his overnight popularity in getting all of England's points in their 21-18 win over Wales. Rob, in fact, went on to appear on the *Wogan* show on the Monday night, by which time I was back in Hawick ready for a hard week's work.

My second appearance on *A Question Of Sport* was in November 1986, this time with Bill Beaumont. I took my son Roddy along with Val and myself by car and Roddy thoroughly enjoyed himself getting autographs of all the celebrities. As in my first appearance, our team lost by one point although this time I answered all my questions correctly. Maybe I'll be in a winning side on a third show.

At any rate it was good to get congratulations about the win over France but I and the rest of the boys were brought down to earth at the training session on the following Sunday when Derrick Grant told us in no uncertain terms that we had been lucky to beat the French. The selectors, though, made only one change in the winning side to play Wales at Cardiff. They dropped Jeremy Campbell-Lamerton and brought in Iain Paxton. I felt sorry for Jeremy who had played so well against France. But apart from everything else Paxton seemed to have a habit which very few people have of scoring tries against Wales.

Our pre-match preparations went well and we stayed as usual at Chepstow before the game, which was played in very windy conditions at the National Stadium in Cardiff. At the interval we were winning by 12-9, although had Gavin kicked as well as he had done against France we really should have been about 20 points up. Much of the trouble was that the kind of rugby ball being used was not the same type as that which he had been kicking to such good effect at Murrayfield, and with the gusting wind I could understand his difficulties. I had a chat with him at the interval and he assured me he felt capable of potting a few in the second-half if the opportunity was offered.

We had a tremendous spell of pressure for about ten minutes in the second-half. In one move Roy Laidlaw took a tap penalty, fed David Sole and the prop went over the line. I was certain it was a try but the New Zealand referee Bob Francis was badly sighted at the penalty and refused the score. Then, from an almost identical situation, Sole again went over the line. He told me later that he had definitely touched down but again no score was given.

Apart from these two "scores" being chalked off, the thing which really broke our hearts was a 70-yard penalty by the Welsh full-back Paul Thorburn. When I saw him take the kick I thought he must be going to find touch, but he elected to go for a penalty goal. The ball seemed to hang for ages in the sky until it finally crossed the bar. Just to add to our misery Thorburn kicked another penalty to make the final tally 22-15 for Wales. But we had scored three tries in Cardiff thanks to Matt Duncan, John Jeffrey and Gavin Hastings, who also kicked one penalty goal, and we had no reason to be despondent about our display.

A fortnight later we were hosts to England at Murrayfield. We made one enforced change because of a facial injury sustained when David Sole was playing for his club Bath against Moseley. Poor David was really sick about missing the Calcutta Cup match but we brought in Alex Brewster who had made the transition from wing-forward to prop.

Most of the newspapers I saw had us written off before we stepped on to the pitch. The English were so confident of their chances that they cancelled the normal Sunday squad session in case their boys were over-trained. One of our local Scottish evening newspapers said in so many words that we were going as lambs to the slaughter, which incensed John Jeffrey so much that he went around all the other players quoting from the article.

Well, nothing inspires a Scot so much as to be written off — especially against England — and in the dressing room on the afternoon of 15 February 1986 I thought to myself, "God help the English."

My confidence in the ability of the team was not misplaced. Within a minute of the start the English giant lock Wade Dooley was knocked flat on the ground by an aggressive-looking John Beattie. Dooley wagged his finger at John who just laughed and from then on it was all Scotland.

England had been confident their heavy pack would drive us back to the Waverley Station, but in fact we scrummaged them off the field. We used the short line-out to such good effect that their lumbering giants were caught completely cold. The score — 33-6 for us — is now part of rugby history and it made everyone in world rugby circles wake up and realise that the Scots were back in championship form. It was the highest score against England since the series began in 1871. Gavin, fully recovered from Wales, scored 21 points with his boot, including conversions of tries by his brother Scott, Matt Duncan and John Rutherford.

No wonder the champagne flowed that night, although I got a bit of a shock when a waiter came up to me and said, "Mr Deans, your room bill for champagne is now £100. Would you like me to stop it?" Like a true Scot I immediately denied all knowledge of the signatures in my name and told him to add it to the SRU bill.

It was disappointing to read a few days after that match the **England skipper Nigel Melville complaining** that Scotland had intimidated and infringed during the fixture. I take the view that if you win, well and good. If you lose it's no use bitching about it.

Our final championship match was of course against Ireland in Dublin. This is never easy and we all knew that as we headed off after the usual build-up in Edinburgh. But as expected wee Roy Laidlaw, who finds Lansdowne Road a happy hunting ground, came up trumps yet again to score a try, while Gavin Hastings kicked two penalty goals to give us a 10-9 win and a share in the title.

The game was as close as the score indicates and indeed Mike Kiernan could have snatched a win for his team had he kicked a late penalty goal. I wouldn't have been terribly happy had that happened but on the other hand it wouldn't have been too bad, for the Scots and Irish boys have a great rugby relationship and the dinner that night was one of the best I've enjoyed.

There was one more big task for the Scottish team to tackle before the season ended for them and that was to visit Bucharest for a win over the Romanians who had beaten our touring side in 1984 at their national stadium by 28-22. This was a one-off match and we flew into Bucharest on the Thursday.

Conditions for the match were pretty good with the temperature around the 70s. John Jeffrey, Scott Hastings and myself all scored tries. But I felt really sorry for Roger Baird who touched down what appeared to be a perfectly good try only to have the score disallowed because the English touch judge, Laurie Prideaux, said his foot had been in touch. Still we ended up with a satisfactory 33-18 victory to avenge the 1984 boys.

I think we were all a bit stunned by the amount of media attention which followed the game. Scots teams have a very high reputation when touring abroad. But on this particular trip that image was somewhat tarnished. The truth is that the food at the official dinner was poor, so a lot of the boys couldn't face it and concentrated instead on the wine and beer. Well, if you've got 21 fit young men who know that if they walk out they're going to be followed by some gun-toting policeman, cooped up in an hotel there's almost bound to be trouble.

There was a bit of horseplay admittedly but no one wrecked the hotel. In fact the majority of people, including the Scots Press boys with us and the officials, heard nothing at all until the following morning when the hotel manager put in a bill for damages.

The Romanians are always desperate for Western currency and they certainly screwed it out of the Scots party. In all, as far as I could gather, four doors, made of balsa wood, had been damaged. That was mainly because the locks didn't work properly and if you get a hefty forward pushing at a balsa wood door something's got to give.

We were in a hopeless position for we couldn't move out of the hotel or country without paying up. The Romanians wanted £800 and at most our officials estimated that £200 would have covered the damage. However we had to stump up or miss our plane and no one fancied staying any longer in Bucharest. At the end of the day the boys concerned paid up. So ended an incident which I submit was blown up out of all proportion.

It had been a great honour for me to captain Scotland in a season which so nearly brought us another Grand Slam. But the icing was put on the cake when I was picked to lead the British Lions against the Rest of the World at Cardiff in April.

I had Gavin Hastings, John Rutherford and John Beattie to help me from Scotland. And of course all the rest of the players were in the highest class. I felt that after 13 years of striving at last I'd made it to the top, for I don't think any player would argue that leading the Lions — even if only at Cardiff instead of a major overseas tour — is the supreme honour.

Our coach for the fixture was that extrovert Irishman Mick Doyle who cheerfully tried the almost impossible task of moulding this collection of individuals into a team in time for the game itself.

The conditions were atrocious, with a downpour of rain at the start making life difficult for anyone who tried to handle the ball. We were edged out by 15-7 at the end of the day, but had bad luck in

One of my proudest moments: Captain of the Lions 1986 at Cardiff v World XV.

losing John Rutherford with a broken nose and Wade Dooley with a knee injury. Our match was on the Wednesday and on the Saturday the Lions, mainly composed of people who had not played in the first match, turned out again at Twickenham to play against an Overseas XV as the Five Nations. A magnificent display of running rugby by the Overseas team, led by my old friend Andy Dalton, saw them win by 32-13.

I had another wee boost when I was picked as No.4 in the *Rugby World* magazine's competition for Player of the Year and yet another when Val and I were invited to Floors Castle near Kelso in the summer to meet the Duchess of Kent. This invitation came through my involvement in helping arrange a charity game for cancer research. Both Val and I thought there would be a big crowd for lunch so we were rather stunned to find half a dozen people waiting for us. "Has everyone else gone in?" I asked. "We're everyone," was the reply. Anyway we were put at our ease and thoroughly enjoyed our visit.

I also received an invitation to attend the Freedom of Glasgow ceremony for Kenny Dalglish. What a nice man he turned out to be and he promised he'd try to get the Scottish football team to emulate the rugby side's performance against England.

So, with no tours to distract me, I had a leisurely summer and

John Rutherford: A world class player and a very good friend. (Courtesy: Bob Thomas)

looked foward to the 1986/87 season. I knew we had a good squad and I was happy that I had found the best way of getting them to respond. If you're captain of anything you have to study individuals. Some guys need a boot up the bottom, others require consideration and mollycoddling. Once you've got the right answer to their individual needs you're on your way to making a team tick.

I find that this pays off not only in rugby but in business. I'm very lucky in my employers and just as lucky in my sales force which includes a guy whom I sometimes play against in club matches, prop Gerry McGuinness of West of Scotland. I'm grateful to all of them for allowing me the time to take part in the greatest sport in the world.

Chapter 15

WEATHER WINS

SEASON 1986/87 promised to be extremely busy. On the domestic front I had a new job — I'd been promoted to sales manager of my firm — I had a new garden to get into shape and I achieved a long standing aim of at last being able to take Val and the boys for our first holiday abroad. All these factors meant I had to call off from any idea of Scotland's five-match tour of Spain and France before the actual season got under way — which turned out to be a bit of a bonus. When I did start training with Hawick the break from rugby gave me a new zest and enthusiasm. Anyway I knew the season was going to be long and hard.

No one was admitting to looking as far ahead as May 1987 and the World Cup but it was obviously at the back of the minds of all the top players. I simply had to be selective in the number of matches I played or I would have been burnt out by the time that came round. For instance, in September 1986 there were no fewer than eight club fixtures and four representative games. So I sat down and decided what matches I could reasonably take part in.

The most important concerned Japan who had an early tour of Scotland and England as part of their World Cup build-up. They started off with a game against the South on 17 September and I had the honour of captaining the boys to a pretty good win in an evening match. The final score was 45-12 in our favour with the South notching up eight tries. Eric Paxton was in particularly good form that night, bursting through dozens of despairing Japanese tackles during the course of the game. Afterwards Shiggy Kono, the touring team's manager, said he was disappointed but not downhearted. "South were a very good side," he added.

But I must admit I had been rather disappointed at the standard of the Japanese play in that match. They have now been playing rugby for 87 years and despite recent wins over the USA and Canada their return from having around 3,000 different clubs — more than any other of the countries playing in the World Cup — has been a bit meagre. That is largely due to the fact that their players as a general rule cannot match the physique of the All Blacks, the Aussies or the Five Nations countries.

Despite the impression given in their game against the South, though, there are indications that at top level Japan could become a real force in the game. We were perhaps lucky to play the tourists before they had really found their feet, for they went on to beat North/Midlands by 27-19, although Edinburgh scored a 26-14 win.

The international — we treated it as a full international although it was labelled a Scotland XV v Japan and no caps were awarded — was at Murrayfield on 27 September. As captain of the Scotland side I soon was grateful for the fact that we had taken the preparations for the game so seriously. For I found we didn't have things by any means going all our own way despite finally winning 33-18. The match was memorable for the fact that Iwan Tukalo, the Selkirk winger, ran in no fewer than four tries. His fellow Borderer, the Kelso stalwart Roger Baird, had been injured and could only look on enviously. At the time Tukalo could only boast one cap — against Ireland in 1985 — and was obviously keen to get back into the international reckoning. Our other tries came from Matt Duncan of West of Scotland who was the other winger and my clubmate and second-row forward Alister Campbell. The scoring was completed by full-back Peter Dods of Gala who kicked three conversions and one penalty goal.

It's always a great psychological boost for any team to get off to a winning start. But as I said, the Japanese showed they were learning all the time. Their scrummaging was solid and they had two good props in Ohta and Aizawa and as usual they tore round the field at a fair rate of knots. For once however Scotland, who suffer just now

166

The Oriental chaps with a future: South v Japan, Melrose, 1986-87 season.

from a lack of authentic second-row forwards and have to use lads who normally play at No.8, were able to dominate the line-out. That was thanks to good work by Iain Paxton, who plays preferably at No.8 but was in the second row that day, and the Glasgow Academical No.8 John Beattie, who had the misfortune to have his right knee ligaments so badly damaged against England in the following Spring that he was out of the World Cup squad.

After the heady atmosphere of Murrayfield it was back to the bread and butter of the national leagues. Hawick's first game was on 4 October and while I was glad we won, I felt a bit sorry that it should be against Jed-forest who had just been promoted and, as all Scotland knows, had the bad luck to be relegated to the second division again when the league season ended in Spring 1987. I have a special affection for Jed as so many of the officials and players, especially Roy Laidlaw the international scrum-half, are friends.

Off the field that month brought one of the biggest honours I've ever had. I was given a civic reception by my home town of Hawick. It was made all the sweeter because only one other individual has had a similar reception and that was Chay Blyth, the famous yachtsman. Incidentally, I often wonder how Chay got into yachting because Hawick can only boast the River Teviot running through it!

I hope he enjoyed his honour as much as I did mine. It was a memorable night for Val and me and my mum and my father who was still alive then. The Provost presented me with a silver salver and six crystal glasses. Five of them were inscribed with the teams I had captained the previous season — Hawick, South of Scotland,

Scotland, Barbarians and Lions. The sixth, I was told, was being left blank until it too could be inscribed 'Scotland's World Cup Captain'. At that time of course I realised there was a lot of mighty hard work to be done if I were to achieve that post.

The night was a tremendous one for me with so many friends turning out in the Town Hall. I was particularly pleased to see Bill McLaren and his wife Betty. Bill was the man who really taught me the basics of rugby at school and set me on the path which was to bring me so much success and friendship in the game. He is a real home-loving man, Bill, and even when he's doing one of his famous commentaries on an international in London, Cardiff or Paris he's off the minute his job is done and on the first plane home. So it was really something for him to accept an invitation to a social function.

On 8 November we took on our old rivals Gala in a league match at Mansfield Park and beat them. Gala were having problems and indeed the unthinkable happened that season with them going down to Division Two for the first time in their proud history. Sad times indeed for a club which has won the Division One title three times.

There have been a lot of theories about what has brought Gala to this unhappy state of affairs. My personal view is that the club adopted the wrong policy in the mid and late 1970s. They recruited players from outside Galashiels, mainly from Edinburgh, and passed over the young Gala men who were playing for their junior sides. Certainly their policy brought success in the early 1980s when they picked up their titles. But now when they need them the more gifted young local players are turning down invitations to become part of the Gala set-up.

On 23 November, a Sunday, I had my second go at the BBC's *A Question of Sport*, as a member of Bill Beaumont's team, then my next non-rugby invitation was to go down to London with John Rutherford to join in the Sportsman of the Year celebrations. Neither John nor I were in the hunt for a personality award (I wonder why?), but it was good to see all the famous sporting faces and mingle with so many sporting stars.

On 1 January 1987 we had our traditional New Year game with Heriot's which we won and in which I scored a try. Because of the fixture it was a quiet and sober New Year. I picked up a good bash in the eye from one of the Heriot's players but I was fine for the trial and, with most of the boys who had caused an upset the previous year now in the Blues or Probables team I captained, we got the right result. By this time winter was really setting in and with pretty well all the grounds in Scotland frozen, the SRU had called for a trial match at Murrayfield to keep the international squad in trim. Thanks to the famous electric blanket, the match went on and it was good to get some kind of a game although Finlay Calder took an ankle knock and Matt Duncan pulled a hamstring.

What a boon the blanket at Murrayfield has been to Scottish rugby, though. It was installed back in 1959 thanks to the generosity of Mr Charles Hepburn, who was in the whisky trade, and there is a well-deserved plaque on the wall near the SRU offices recording his gift.

Even so, all our preparations were to prove in vain for on 14 January the whole of Britain was in the grip of some of the worst weather known and, because of the impossibility of spectators getting safely to the ground, the match against England at Twickenham was put off. The Wales v Ireland fixture at Cardiff suffered the same fate. As both Finlay and Matt had been very doubtful there were mixed feelings about the postponement. Certainly the weather had improved somewhat by 17 January, the date fixed for the match. But if anyone had been killed getting to Twickenham I'm sure the Rugby Union would have felt profound guilt. So it was a hard decision to make but I feel personally it was the right one.

The other point was that you couldn't put your mind to thinking about preparations for the big game because you wondered how you were going to get to Murrayfield for the Thursday training session, let alone get to Twickenham. Indeed Bill Hogg, the SRU secretary, was thinking of getting a helicopter to pick up the Border boys, but thankfully that wasn't required and I had a weekend at home, as did all the other players.

The following Saturday we had a vital league match against Kelso at Mansfield Park. We were unbeaten at the time and needed only to win to pretty well tie up another championship title. However Kelso, whose only defeat of the season had been by Boroughmuir, had obviously given a lot of thought to the match. They attacked us at our weakest points and adopted ploys like stacking their jumpers at the tail of the line-out which threw us out of our stride. Still we got off to a good start and I think we would have won had not our prop Stewart Hogg lost the ball, after selling a dummy, as he crossed the line near the interval.

YOU'RE A HOOKER, THEN

Kelso played well, no doubt about it, and they also had luck on their side. For example Andrew Ker, their stand-off, tried for a penalty goal which hit the cross-bar, fell down on my head and bounced back to our full-back John Hogg. It all happened so quickly that poor John dropped the ball over the line, thus conceding a five-metre scrum. We were penalised at that and this time Ker made no mistake with his penalty kick.

The final score was 18-12 for Kelso and now we knew we had to win all our remaining fixtures and try and get a better points differential to hang on to the title. I'm glad to say we managed that, our final game being a 20-12 win over Watsonians, again at Mansfield Park. So we had our fourth title in a row. But it was certainly a nail-biting league campaign.

The following week after the Kelso match the weather turned sour again and once more the Murrayfield blanket was switched on. The B team had a game against France B at St Andrews coming up so they played against the full Scotland side. With hindsight it was probably not the best of ideas. The B boys were well beaten and France inflicted a 15-9 defeat against them the following week.

That was a particularly sad week for me. I was down with 'flu and missed a match against Jed-forest in which Alister Campbell had his jaw broken, but more important my father, who had been forced to retire early from work because of a series of heart attacks, died. He was a very popular man who had hooked for Hawick in the late 1940s and his death was a great loss to me personally.

But life must go on.

With Alister injured, a fellow Hawick player, Alan Tomes, was brought back into the Scottish team for our game against Ireland at Murrayfield on 21 February 1987. Alan had been playing well all season but Alister had got the call probably because he had been in the side which shared the championship the previous season.

When I led the boys out against the Irish I was equalling the world record number of caps (45) for a hooker which had been held by the greatly respected Irishman Dr Ken Kennedy. I don't care about records — I'm just proud to go out and play for my country and captaining such a good set of players is reward enough. I had started off with the ambition of playing once for Scotland. To have played 45 times in the same position was fantastic.

In the dressing room before we left there was a touching moment for me when I mentioned my dad's death. John Rutherford, who

170

It's amazing what these Kelso men will do to win the game.

attended the funeral, told the boys that was the first time I'd mentioned the death all weekend and he thought that was worth a win in memory of my father.

Chapter 16

WIN SOME — LOSE SOME

THE build-up to the Ireland game of 1987 — one in which two exceptionally exciting sides were prepared to play an open game . . . and did just that — was fairly typical.

On the Wednesday night I went through my usual procedure. I cleaned my boots in the kitchen, got the family to kiss them for good luck, then I packed them along with my training gear, my No.1 track suit for the Friday photographic session and my actual playing kit. The SRU are sticklers for the right gear — Umbro track suits and Adidas footwear. Even in the Braid Hills Hotel before a game we have to wear the Adidas training shoes. I packed the kids off to bed, answered a few phone calls from the Press boys looking for quotes before the game and settled down to watch football on television. The game was Scotland v Republic of Ireland and the result did nothing for my morale. It was a 1-0 defeat for Scotland.

Next morning Roddy was looking for a lift to school and he was full of "Good luck, Dad". I tell you, if Scotland had scored a try for every good luck wish I received that week, we would have won by about 200 points.

I got on the road and it was like going down to Mansfield Park or going off to war . . . I don't think there can be a lot of difference. Around 9.15 a.m. I picked up team-mate Greig Oliver, our Hawick

Ready for the 1986-87 campaign.

scrum-half who was as nervous as a kitten, this being his first taste of
life at the rugby top. He was to sit on the bench for Roy
Laidlaw, the Scotland veteran. After that up the road to Clovenfords,
where Peter Dods of Gala was waiting, and on to Edinburgh.

The boys had a good work out at Murrayfield and there was a note
of determination in the camp that we in rugby would avenge the
Scottish soccer defeat. Then it was back to the hotel for a good meal
and early to bed.

On the Friday there was a buzz going around that Trevor
Ringland was doubtful and that gave us a boost. That night we went
to the cinema to see *Crocodile Dundee* and all the boys seemed to enjoy
it. So did I, but I ended up paying for all the ice-creams — about 23
of them!

The day of the match dawned. Around 11 a.m. the forwards and
backs met separately and then got together around 15 minutes later.
Lunch was available, for those who could face it, between 11.30 and
11.45 a.m. One thing I've noticed recently is that Mars bars figure a
lot on these lunch menus, the chocolate being reckoned to give an
energy boost.

We got to the ground on a perfect day with the pitch in marvellous

173

condition. Our Five Nations campaign had been delayed for weeks because of the cancellation of the England game, whereas Ireland already had a winning match under their belt. But in the Scots dressing room there was a wonderful air of confidence. Every player seemed to feel about ten feet tall and when we went out on to the ground the crowd roared us on. They were really right behind us. My heart was thumping but I had a winning feeling.

Within five minutes of the match starting John Rutherford put us ahead with a drop goal. Then we began to control the game with some lethal kicking by the same player. The Scots were by now giving the Irish a lesson on rucking and Rutherford again was amongst the points with a second drop goal.

So we were 6-0 ahead. But it seems to be a common failing amongst Scots in any sport that once we are ahead we are inclined to sit back, almost as though we're sorry for the opposition and want to give them a chance. That happened here when in the first real Irish attacking move Bill Lenihan crashed over for a try, with Michael Kiernan converting. Then Kiernan dropped a goal and we were behind by 9-6.

First-half injury time, and a high ball was kicked into the Irish 22. Both Iain Milne and David Sole did some lovely driving to suck in the Irish forwards and the ball was finally presented perfectly for Roy Laidlaw to accept and gleefully cross for a try which put us 10-9 ahead with everything still to play for. I must admit my thoughts were what the hell was going to happen. But I couldn't complain. Everything had gone to plan except that fatal lack of concentration which had cost us six points.

We started to take command again in the second-half. Gavin Hastings at full-back didn't have his kicking boots on and both he and Michael Kiernan missed a few pots at goal. Ringland, rumours about whose fitness had been greatly exaggerated, put in some sterling tackles which prevented us increasing our slender lead.

However, continuous pressure was kept on the Irish and in particular by that old and well-tried combination of Rutherford and Laidlaw. It was Rutherford who made a decisive break. Paul Dean and Hugo MacNeill were caught out when he kicked and Iwan Tukalo quickly pounced on the loose ball for a try which Hastings converted. From then on, despite Kiernan clawing back three points with a penalty goal, we were 110 per cent in control of the game. At the short line-outs especially, Tomes and Iain Paxton were immense. Our scrummaging was first-class, with again much of the credit going to The Bear whose fellow prop David Sole followed every loose ball. Our back row snapped up every chance, the old firm of Rutherford and Laidlaw were on song and there was no lack of elation and joy in the dressing room afterwards.

Sure, we had a few points to sharpen up on, but it was a time for celebration. I think most of us are a bit sorry when Ireland are our victims — maybe it's our Celtic blood, for apart from a few Irishmen I encountered halfway round the world in 1983, I've always had a special place in my heart for the Irish team and players.

The dinner that night was the usual grand affair in an Edinburgh hotel. But my mind went back to the Irish dinner given at the Shelbourne in Dublin after our Triple Crown win there in 1984. Over the past few years the Irish dinners have been the best in the rugby calendar. They know how to enjoy themselves and so do we. There's a special feeling at the Shelbourne with Scots and Irish fans mingling together.

On that famous Triple Crown night Laidlaw and I turned up wearing bow ties which flashed. They'd been presented to us by the huge English lock Maurice Colclough during the 1983 Lions tour. Colclough called us the Scottish gnomes. Anyway, our ties flashed away merrily until we and the rest of the lads were summoned to appear in a *Sportscene* TV special with Bill McLaren and Dougie Donnelly. Coach Jim Telfer spotted the ties and growled, "Get them off. We'll have no Mickey Mouse ties here." But the interviews seemed to go down well. Jim Aitken, our captain, got a bit of stick from the boys during his stint and we finished up singing *Bonnie Mary of Argyll*.

After a few pints we boarded the bus for our hotel which was about 20 miles out of town and the boys were pretty shattered by then. We found the bar was closed when we did get back so it was a pretty quiet ending to an historic evening and of course our thoughts then were on meeting France in a couple of weeks time in the Grand Slam encounter at Murrayfield.

The next memorable dinner in Ireland was in 1985/86 season when we sneaked through as winners by 10-9, thereby contributing to Ireland's whitewash. They readily forgave us and the dinner was a hoot.

It all started with that likeable Ulsterman Willie Anderson declaring that the table he was sitting at was a 'no cutlery' area. That meant from the start of the meal, which was soup, to the end, which was fresh fruit salad and cream, no one could use a spoon or knife and fork. I don't know if you've ever tried to eat a meal without cutlery . . . personally I've seen pigs doing it more daintily than these rugby characters. Well, after that the usual quiet sedate dinner was forgotten, with we Scots celebrating our share of the championship and the Irish drowning their sorrows after taking the wooden spoon. But it was hard to tell us apart, so great is the friendship between the players of both teams.

I think this is really the one worthwhile advertisement for the game of rugby. You get 30 players who have been engaged for 80 minutes in mentally and physically sapping rugby and in a hard, aggressive contact sport sitting down as the best of friends.

After Scotland's 1987 win over Ireland we in the Hawick side had a vital league match against our near neighbours Selkirk. Every point counted now that we were on the one defeat mark along with Kelso. Fortunately for us, Selkirk were without their international half-backs, Gordon Hunter and John Rutherford, on the day and we ran out winners by a good margin which helped boost our differential.

On the international front the papers were full of the forthcoming match with France in Paris on 7 March. There was a good deal of speculation because France, although they had beaten both England and Wales, had been none too impressive and either of the home countries might have won. But I knew that France in Paris, playing their third game of the season, would have settled down by now and would be very difficult to beat. Meantime it was good to have the Scottish selectors pick the same side which had beaten Ireland. Consistency is a great thing in rugby and we were beginning to play like a good club side.

The Sunday training session went well and Tuesday found me up north on business at Coylum Bridge where my company was holding an exhibition. That evening we decided to take a dip in the hotel pool after the day's work. On my way to the pool one of the attendants stopped me and asked if I played rugby. When I asked why he said, "We think we know who you are." At last, I thought, here's fame. I'm recognised even in Coylum Bridge. "Who am I?" I asked. "We think you're Iain Milne," was the deflating reply. Gerry McGuinness happened to be with me and he certainly didn't let me down lightly over that one!

At the usual Thursday session we had a gruelling three hours training and everything went marvellously well. The tactics were worked out and we headed for Paris determined to lay the bogey of the Parc des Princes. Before we left the airport one of the journalists came up to me and asked if I thought 36-year-old Milne would be able to stick out the pace in Paris. I was sure he meant Alan Tomes, the veteran lock, but he insisted on Milne being 36 which promptly earned The Bear the title Papa Bear on the journey.

Once we got to our hotel, well outside Paris, the President of the Maison Lafitte club where we always train before a match came along with a photographer and asked for his friend "Colin, the captain of Scotland". That was the signal for Iain Milne who passed himself off as me and proudly posed for photographs with the President.

The same thing happened next day after our training session at the Maison Lafitte sports ground where the local mayor handed over a presentation to the Scottish captain, alias Iain Milne. It was all a bit puzzling for the Scottish Press corps who must have wondered if I had been deposed, but the boys enjoyed the self-promotion of The Bear.

After training and a leisurely lunch some of us went on to a nearby racecourse and stayed for the first race and then it was back to our hotel to prepare mentally for next day's match. About 6 p.m. we had what we call the senior pros meeting. This simply means that some of the senior players like The Bear, Roy Laidlaw, John Rutherford and myself sit down with the coaches, Derrick Grant and Ian McGeechan, and discuss the next day's game. We go over the tactics, decide on what we'll try and do, attempt to work out where things can go wrong and why, and generally build up a mental picture of the way we envisage what might happen. Then it was early to bed and next day another spine-chilling bus ride into Paris with the motor cycle escort ignoring red lights, traffic and pedestrians.

It was another lovely day, if on the cold side. One thing which really heartened me and the rest of the boys was when we took the customary pre-match stroll on to the pitch. There was a crowd of Scots fans already in the ground and as we stepped out into the middle of the awesome Parc des Princes they burst into *Flower of Scotland*. I thought my heart would jump out of my chest. There was a feeling of pride amongst the whole team and we knew that we had support come hail, rain or shine. What a tremendous sensation.

At last the preliminaries were over and we went out with the exhortations of our President, Doug Smith, ringing in our ears. It's nice to have a President like Doug who has been through it all himself and who is eager to have success for his team.

The game itself was one I'll never forget. We felt confident but the French were in the mood to entertain their support and when they're like that they're simply immense. We pulled out all the stops to try and contain them but it was impossible not to admire their play. Little Berbizier, the scrum-half, was all over the field, feeding often to his back row where Eric Champ in particular put in some bruising breenges. However we did manage to delay a French score until Doug Wyllie had to go off to get stitches put in a nose injury. Finlay Calder, the flanker, had to fill in on the wing while Doug was off and Laurent Rodriguez won good line-out ball. He passed to Denis Charvet who in turn sent Eric Bonneval away for a try at the corner.

We hit back briefly when John Beattie anticipated a kick by Serge Blanco resulting from a high ball by John Rutherford, and charged it down, going over for a try. But Frank Mesnel dropped a goal with Daniel Dubroca doing his usual ploy of playing at scrum-half at the line-out where the French had a big advantage. Again Bonneval was in the scoring when Gavin Hastings and Matt Duncan collided going for him and the winger got his second try.

The French extended their lead when Blanco sent Philippe Berot over for a similar score and it was a relief to us when Gavin Hastings kicked a penalty goal after he had been high-tackled by Pascal Ondarts. Before the interval, however, Berot also got a penalty goal to make it 18-7 and a distinctly gloomy prospect for us.

The second-half opened disastrously. A long pass by Charvet went to ground but that man Bonneval was quick to pounce on it and go over the line. There were about three Scots near Bonneval and we were all so convinced that he had knocked on that we relaxed. That was an expensive lesson we learned — always play to the whistle no matter how sure you are . . . and I'm sure he did knock on.

So what do you say to the boys when you're 22-7 down and still a long way to go? All you can do is coax them along. In this case they certainly responded.

Gavin Hastings kicked a penalty goal before Berot did the same for France. But as the final quarter came we threw caution to the winds. We spread the ball to keep the French running from side to side and it soon began to show. We dominated in that last quarter,

Two of the best — Rud and Sella.

which saw Keith Robertson come on for Wyllie who had eventually to retire with concussion. He added some flair to the centre play.

A wickedly placed kick by John Rutherford behind the French backs saw Gavin Hastings striding up, grabbing the ball and sending brother Scott over for a try. Despite the fact that the ball toppled over as he made his run-up, Gavin managed to hit the top of it and it sneaked over the bar for a successful conversion. Gavin added a penalty goal to make it 25-19 before Berot got a similar score when one of our boys was offside. We were still plugging away, still attacking and Gavin kicked yet another penalty to make it 28-22.

We ended on a high note and had Finlay Calder managed to hold on to a bouncing ball on the French line we'd have scored. But the final whistle — a sound not one of the Scots boys wanted to hear — went, with France hugely relieved to hang on to their 28-22 victory.

It was a joy of a game in which to take part and a great deal of the credit goes to the New Zealand referee, Keith Lawrence, who handled his first really big match with all the aplomb of a veteran. There was no dirty play, no disputed decisions and everyone who saw it will remember it for many a long year. We had given it our best shot but had just failed and in the dressing room afterwards, while all the boys were disappointed not to have won, they knew they had put in a worthy effort. 007 — James Bond, otherwise known as Scot Sean Connery — came into the dressing room to see us and said how proud he had been to be a Scot that day.

The dinner at the Grand that evening was a very quiet affair. I think all the boys were shattered by their exertions on the field. However we got singing at last and The Bear took over the proceedings in his own inimitable manner, giving his rendition of *Father Abraham*.

Later that week I was doing an interview with Bill McLaren about the match and he told me that down in Wales they were replacing their planned video showing of the 1973 All Blacks v Barbarians game with the France-Scotland match of 1987, quite a compliment from the valley viewers.

Our next international was against Wales but before that Hawick had a vital league match against Boroughmuir at Meggatland. We only had about three regular first-team members available and were given little chance. But the game had to be won if we were to stay in touch for the championship title and with the new boys playing their part we won 28-19 in a match where I managed to grab a try.

The following Sunday the international squad were on duty again for training at Murrayfield. Wyllie couldn't be considered because of injury so the experienced Robertson remained while Alan Tomes, who had tendon trouble, was replaced by Derek White, the Gala captain and normally a No.8 and not a second-row man. Indeed all of our back five for the Welsh match were composed of players who usually were No.8 forwards for their clubs.

At the training session Derrick Grant lost no time in telling us that we were no world beaters and that a team was only as good as its last game . . . and for us that had been a defeat. Well, you don't get much chance to get swell-headed in the Scottish rugby side! The training went smoothly, with Keith Robertson and Derek White slotting in without any problem. The forwards were scrummaging well and it was a morale booster to us that we pushed two tons on the scrum machine. Another boost came later that week when we heard that Stuart Evans, the Welsh equivalent of our own mighty Bear, had

The Bear shows his slip.

failed a late fitness test, to be replaced by the comparatively unknown Peter Francis of Maesteg.

Since I had first been made captain of the side I used to visit all the lads in their rooms after Saturday lunch, stressing the importance of each individual's task. But on this particular Saturday of the Welsh game that back-fired on me. The boys had got used to my room calls and when I knocked on the door of the room shared by John Beattie and John Jeffrey I heard a muffled voice saying, "Is that you, Dino?" I went into the room and all I could hear was giggling . . . it was the two Johns hiding under the blankets and acting like schoolboys. So the serious side of the game was forgotten for the moment anyway.

We had a special guest for the match — Princess Anne, who was accompanied by her son, Peter — so we left the hotel a wee bit earlier than usual. There was a good atmosphere, with singing on the bus and as we walked into the dressing room. The usual format had been changed a bit and the team picture was earlier. Then about 2 p.m.

181

we were introduced to Princess Anne, whom I found absolutely delightful, and her son, who showed tremendous interest for a boy so young. Before we went back inside I was able to look up into the stand and see Val and Roddy. Val had earlier been to a lunch attended by the Princess and was thrilled about that.

When we took to the pitch, for the first time ever the band played a really Scottish anthem, *Scotland The Brave*, but I must admit we didn't sing that. We sang *Flower of Scotland* which is the song we're really at home with.

We were champing at the bit. The whistle went and the game was under way.

From the very first scrum we pushed the Welsh pack back and we knew that pyschologically they were missing Evans badly. We pushed so well that we got within ten metres of their line before there was another scrum. We had remembered how the Aussies in their 1985 Grand Slam tour had taken on the Welsh at Cardiff and scored a pushover try. So when we got down my call to the boys was "Aussie". The Bear and his fellow prop David Sole put on a push which must have sent a shudder through every Welshman present at Murrayfield and we scored our first international pushover try, Beattie being credited with the actual touch down and Gavin Hastings converting.

We didn't look back after that and tore holes in the Welsh defence. Gavin managed only two penalty goals out of five attempts — one in front of the posts — and Jonathan Davies, the Welsh stand-off, dropped a goal. Near the interval John Rutherford broke clear through the Welsh defence and gave to Finlay Calder. Finlay, all arms and legs, shook off the Welsh and fired out a takeable pass to John Jeffrey. But with the line at his mercy John dropped the ball. I was sorry we had missed that chance of a possible six points but well pleased with the way things were going in general.

My half-time team talk was for a little more composure in our finishing. We were rushing around at 100 m.p.h. but we were also trying to finish off moves at that speed. Still, we were well up in all sections of the game and particularly in the scrummaging. However within a minute of the restart Mark Wyatt kicked a penalty goal, then added another, to reduce our lead to three points. We had seemed to go to sleep after the interval.

After that we clawed our way back into the game. It was John Rutherford who gave us a nice cushion of points again with a drop goal — his 12th for Scotland — and it could not have come at a better time. Then Finlay Calder, the man of the match that day, I reckon, broke away and passed to Matt Duncan. He was held but got the ball out to Jeffrey who crossed for an easy try. Gavin converted with the most difficult kick of the afternoon, having missed two much easier ones earlier on.

It wasn't until the match was into about the sixth minute of injury time that the Welsh got a decent handling move together and Mark Jones touched down a try for Wyatt to convert. But we had won by 21-15 and we all knew that the Triple Crown was still there to be won.

Before that date at Twickenham against England on 4 April, on which the season's honours depended, Hawick were involved again in the league championship title. We had won that for the previous three seasons and I had the trophy in my home. The Hawick President phoned me to ask me to take the trophy up to Murrayfield at our next Saturday training session so that it could be whipped down to whoever won, Kelso or ourselves. He also asked me to put the base of the trophy into the jewellers to be inscribed. As I was in a bit of a hurry I just handed it in, asking that the inscription be engraved. To my horror, when I collected it, I found that the jeweller had inscribed it — season 1986/87 winners Hawick. I was in a real sweat. Here we were, winners according to the trophy but we still had to play the final match. So I stalled for time and tried to ignore the phone calls from the SRU asking that the base be delivered. I don't know what drastic measures I would have had to have taken had we lost. But fortunately for all concerned we beat Watsonians by 20-12 and our points differential ensured we had the title again.

So thoughts were now on the Triple Crown bid at Twickenham against England who had banned four of their players for their actions on the field in the match against Wales. What worried me was that everyone in the media seemed to expect us to win easily. We had been in the same position so often before and I knew things could go badly wrong. A caged and cornered animal is a dangerous one and that's what this England side was. However we had played three very good games of rugby already and we only had the one enforced change, Roger Baird coming into the centre for Scott Hastings who had had the bad luck to fracture his cheekbone against Wales.

Conditions for the match were exactly the opposite to what I wanted. It rained and rained and there was no sign of the spring weather we had hoped for. Things went badly from the start. I won the toss of the coin with the new England captain, Mike Harrison, and elected to kick, but Gavin kicked badly and we were put back into our own half.

Full marks to England. They forced line-outs by kicking and we couldn't control this aspect of the game. Things brightened a little when Gavin popped over a penalty goal but Marcus Rose countered with another to equalise. Then Harrison kicked through. Matt Duncan tackled him but he had got rid of the ball and a penalty try, converted by Rose, resulted.

Half-time came with England six points ahead. We lost Beattie with leg ligament trouble and Alan Tomes came on. Because Tomes is such an experienced second-row man we did begin to win some line-out ball but not enough to change the pattern of the game which England had set. Rose kicked a penalty goal, then came the killer punch when the same player kicked, the ball bounced into his hands and he went over for the easiest of tries, converting it himself. When you're playing well everything seems to fall into place for you, including any luck that's going.

Both Gavin and Rose kicked penalty goals. By this time we were running any ball we could get and finally Keith Robertson notched a try, Gavin converting. However England had won 21-12 and I don't think I've ever felt so dejected in my life. A golden opportunity had gone up in smoke . . . or rather in the rain.

It was the sixth time Scotland had gone to Twickenham with the Triple Crown ready to be won and the sixth time we had failed to do so. It seemed such hard luck on the boys who had worked so hard for so many months. But you've got to keep going and after a few words from Doug Smith at the President's reception we began to buck up. At the official dinner I sat beside Colin Cowdray, the great England cricketer. The English were perfect hosts and if the team did blow their own trumpet a bit I think they were entitled to do so.

Next morning when I flew back to Edinburgh with Val I had to wait quite a while for my luggage and got chatting to Bob Munro, the World Cup tour manager. He told me I'd been selected as captain of Scotland's World Cup squad so that was compensation for what had been the saddest rugby day of my life.

Although our Five Nations championship campaign was now over we still had one more match, against Spain at Murrayfield on 19 April 1987. It was unusual for it was played on a Sunday and also because it involved both countries in their first World Cup build-up. The game itself was a difficult one. We were without Iain Milne, John Beattie, John Rutherford and Scott Hastings, all on the injured list. And of course none of the players, with their thoughts on the World Cup, wanted to be injured so for once we didn't have 100 per cent commitment.

I think we were expected to overwhelm the Spanish but in fact their tackling held us to only a four-point lead by the interval. Gavin Hastings opened the scoring with a penalty goal but Spain's stand-off Francisco Puertas equalised with another. Eventually Iwan Tukalo squeezed in at the corner for a try after the Spaniards' tackling had earlier foiled him, Keith Robertson and Gavin when they had gone for the line.

Immediately after the interval we put a better face on things with the pack driving the Spanish scrum back and Iain Paxton got the touch down, Gavin converting. Then in the final quarter, we started to turn it on with Gavin giving a good pass to Robertson. He was held ten metres from the line but got his pass out to John Jeffrey who in turn shot the ball out to me and I crossed for a try, Gavin kicking the conversion. Five minutes later good handling by several of the Scots ended in Matt Duncan, the powerful winger, breaking two Spanish tackles as he tore over for our final try, with Gavin again bringing out full points.

Give the Spaniards their due, they never gave up, and were rewarded in the fifth minute of injury time when their No.8 Alberto Malo sent prop Jose de Moral in for a try to make the final score 25-7 in our favour.

We had a couple of training sessions for the squad in the following weeks — one at St Andrews which made a nice break from constantly going to Murrayfield — and then concentrated on keeping fit before leaving for World Cup duties.

Looking back on the season it was one where we could so easily have accomplished something to make all Scots proud had it not been for falling at the last hurdle. But we had taken part in the three most exciting games in the championship. Most of all we now had a team which blended well, played well and scored tries well. It was a team which I felt privileged to be allowed to lead and of course the icing on the cake was to be chosen as the first World Cup skipper of Scotland.

Chapter 17

WORLD CUP BUILD-UP

PREPARATIONS for the World Cup really got under way on Friday, 24 April. That marked the first official meeting of the squad which was to make the journey to New Zealand. It turned out to be a glorious start with the sun shining as I left Hawick with Greig Oliver and picked up Peter Dods on the way to the Old Course Hotel at St Andrews. The management had decided, rightly, that the boys could do with a break from Murrayfield for their training session.

A few hours before we sat down to dinner Jeremy Campbell-Lamerton went through a fitness test for he was the best man at his brother's wedding in London and had to get away for that. Then we had a get-together about the various timetables for our journey and when the talking stopped and all our questions had been answered Bill Hogg, the SRU secretary, solemnly announced a message from Sir Hector Monro MP, one time sports minister and SRU President of a few years ago. It was to the effect that we could apply for postal votes if we were out of the country at the time of the election. The boys howled at that one. The last thing on our minds at that stage was voting. The only votes we wanted to count were Scottish points scored.

I shared a room with John Rutherford who had the bad luck to receive a knee ligament injury while taking part in an unauthorised

The Bear: what he doing there? (Courtesy: Bob Thomas)

game in Bermuda along with fellow squad members Iain Paxton, Matt Duncan and Iwan Tukalo. It was the kind of injury John could have got playing with his little son. But he and the others knew that the SRU would not have granted them official permission to play in the sun and they had sneaked out the back door. However John and the others were still very much part of the squad and everyone was hoping that our first-choice stand-off would be fully fit by the time we met France.

Next morning we met early in the foyer and had a 20-minute run before breakfast, jogging along the beach. After breakfast it was down to hard work with Ian McGeechan putting us through our speed tests. We had to do 8 × 50 metre sprints then 10 × 100 metres and I'm glad to say I managed them all pretty well, before we finished off with some hard scrummaging.

The afternoon was free and some of the boys took advantage of the magnificent golfing on offer at St Andrews. I couldn't join in as I had to catch up with some business paper work. In the evening we were taken to sample the indoor facilities of St Andrews University and played some cricket — which my team won — and football. Then it

187

was a late dinner back at the hotel and off to bed.

During the Saturday activities Iain 'The Bear' Milne had pulled a muscle — fortunately not a serious injury — while Keith Robertson had stubbed his toe playing football. We were kitted out with our tour blazers and trousers before dispersing for home on Sunday. There was an air almost of desperation to get fit and do well. Everyone wanted to train hard, and everyone did, for we didn't know what might lie ahead of us.

Our next real get-together was at Murrayfield on 1 May. Before that we had been training, the South contingent under Derrick Grant at Jedburgh and the Edinburgh and District boys under Doug Morgan in the Capital. I was frustrated at the Murrayfield training session for after half an hour, while doing a long striding exercise, I pulled a thigh muscle and couldn't participate further. The session ended with the usual press-ups and I did more than was asked for in an effort to make up for that lost training.

Next day, 3 May, was my 32nd birthday but no one twigged and it was another hard training session after the official team photograph for New Zealand had been taken. I still couldn't run but I was able to throw the ball into the line-out and carried out my scrummaging chores, so at least I took some part in the proceedings. We had by now been kitted out with the rest of our tour gear — track suits, shirts, etc — and I must say the SRU did us very well.

I got home around 4 p.m. to find Val had ordered a special birthday cake for me. It was made in the shape of the two New Zealand islands, iced in green for Hawick colours and with the Scottish flag at the bottom. I was very touched — that was typical of Val. Anyway, I can tell you it wasn't long before Roddy and Ross had demolished the islands.

On Wednesday 13 May I started packing for the big adventure. Val took Ross off to her sister's and Roddy was at school, so I had everything ready in a couple of hours. It was Ross's birthday on 15 May but because I would be away Val brought it forward to that night.

We took the boys with a couple of their cousins and some other friends down to the local leisure centre for a birthday party. There was sausage, egg and chips all round, followed by a cake, and we got home around 7 p.m. The mini-bus to take the local South boys up to Edinburgh was due 30 minutes later and I don't think I've ever spent a longer half hour. When it did come I said my farewells to Val, who had a tear in her eye, the boys, who took it all in their stride, and my mum and brother. The whole street seemed to be out to wish me good luck and I made sure I had the team's supply of Hawick Balls, a local sweet which is highly prized in the Borders. The squad met up at an Edinburgh hotel, had a couple of beers and went to bed early for an early rise next day.

The World Cup journey really got on the road, or rather in the sky, on 14 May. At the airport a lot of the wives and sweethearts were present. I was glad I'd said my farewells the previous night — I don't think I could have done it at the airport. There were the usual Press and TV interviews before we were on our way to Gatwick where we swopped into our track suits, ideal for long journeys, and got on the plane for New Zealand.

The flight was due to take 28 hours with a stop for re-fuelling at Los Angeles first of all. It was pretty boring but fortunately I sat beside Finlay Calder who is always a cheery guy to travel with. The Irish and Welsh teams were on the same plane so we chatted to them and also to our President, Doug Smith. We were allowed into the flight deck and it all looked pretty complicated to me, but the pilot assured me it was easy to fly his Jumbo 747. I'll take his word for it.

At L.A. we were off the plane for an hour while re-fuelling was carried out and the same procedure was gone through at Honolulu. With the aid of sleeping pills we had all managed some rest, but I find that you can't sleep comfortably in a plane. Either you wake up with a sore neck, a sore back or both.

Anyway we all chirped up as we got near Auckland. We queued up to shave and got into our official tour outfit of blazer, trousers, etc. We were actually 30 minutes ahead of schedule but the pilot said because of poor visibility we were third in line to land. We eventually did try to get down but the plane had to bank steeply and the landing was aborted. Visibility was nil, so we had to fly to Christchurch to get more fuel, sit around in the plane for a couple of hours and then go back to Auckland. By this time there was no food left and we had finished nearly all the soft drinks. In all we had spent some 40 hours travelling since leaving Edinburgh. We were dead tired but there was still the business of going through Customs and having our boots washed because of an old foot and mouth scare.

At last we got to our hotel and booked in. But within an hour we were on the bus again, heading for an allegedly light training spin. We had done a couple of laps of a nearby pitch when the chasing boys asked the front runners to go a bit easier. Derrick Grant rounded on them and told them not to be lazy. My first thoughts were "Heaven help us". But we were there to win the World Cup and 100 per cent commitment was needed.

We didn't need any rocking to sleep that night.

Next day, 17 May, we had a really hard training session and practised about 40 scrummages against the Irish pack. Then we had some line-out work. But the session ended disastrously when Scott Hastings, the centre, who had been getting over a cheekbone fracture sustained against Wales, suddenly collapsed when running full out. I thought he had torn a hamstring and the boys' heads went down. However the medical opinion was that the injury might not be as serious as at first thought and there were hopes then that he would be able to play against our first opponents, France.

There was an official dinner that night which frankly was a bit of a bore. We could hardly keep our eyes open. But we did get our World Cup caps dished out. They are similar to the normal international caps but are embroidered "World Cup 1987" and have the World Cup logo on one of the panels.

On the Monday we flew to Christchurch. We were to be accompanied, to our amazement, by the French team! We had arrived half an hour before our flight was due, dressed in our No. 1 tour outfit of blazer, flannels, shirt, tie and black shoes and the squad looked pretty smart. The French turned up only ten minutes before take-off, all wearing casual leather jackets, Lee Cooper sponsored jeans and each clutching a personal compact disc hi-fi. On the flight, there was an empty seat beside The Bear and myself so we had the pleasure of the company of prop Jean-Pierre Garuet. Suffice to say, very few words were exchanged in any language!

When we got to our hotel in the suburb of Hornby we found it wasn't quite finished — joiners and electricians were still at work. But the staff were exceptionally nice and, more important for rugby players, the food was very good. We trained as usual and for the first time I managed that afternoon to dash off a letter to Val and the boys — interrupted yet again by another training stint. Later we held a quiz and that turned into an excellent evening with all the players becoming involved.

I didn't sleep well that night — my time clock wasn't working properly after the long journeys we had had — but after a good morning's training in very wet conditions we were able to go duck

Who said it's nice and sunny Down Under?

shooting, or at least Peter Dods and myself did. The local farmer was the father of Andrew Stokes, the boy who had become the Lions mascot in 1983, so it was good to see the family again. As Pete and I were two of the lighter fellows in the squad we were taken on a four-wheeled-drive motor cycle to a pond where the ducks congregated. It was quite a journey and we hung on like grim death, fearful of being thrown off. I had the honour of the first shot. I missed, but later I did bag a bird which brought me the Top Shot medal from Finlay Calder.

Thank goodness that night I at last got a decent sleep and woke up on the morning of 20 May much refreshed. We concentrated that day on scrummage practice which we badly needed. The scrummaging machine provided however was a pretty Mickey Mouse affair with two oil drums as weights. But eventually we had about a dozen people, including the Press boys, plus the drums piled on to the machine and we were shoving pretty well. Later there was the usual throwing-in session and then we watched the first-half again of our match with France in Paris which underlined how difficult they would be to take on. We did get a bit of a boost though when we heard the ace French winger Bonneval was out, although his replacement Esteve was also world-class.

I'm always touched and amazed by the welcome Scots get in New Zealand. Clubs and individuals go to all sorts of trouble to make you feel at home. As an instance, I remember getting a call that night from a Scot who had been 20 years in New Zealand and ran a fish and chip restaurant. Would any of the boys like to come over and try them he asked? When I asked him if he had any haggis he said in all seriousness that he thought he could make some or procure some. Talk about home from home!

But of course at this time we had more on our plates than the prospect of fish and chips . . . or even haggis. The crunch day was rapidly approaching and on 21 May we started off our final preparations by going to jail. There were two reasons for this — one was privacy but more important the weather was absolutely terrible, with rain cascading down and a strong wind blowing, and we hoped the prison walls would give a little shelter. It was so bad that I approached Derrick Grant and suggested we put off the session until the afternoon but the iron man just grunted that it might be as bad then, so we soldiered on and had a good hour's session.

Of course we met the inevitable Scot, ex-Melrose rugby player "Hoss" Smith who had been out there for about eight years and was a prison warder. So after the training we had a cup of tea and a guided tour of the prison. It was interesting but not particularly edifying to see the murderers, child molesters, thieves and so on who made up the prison population and I think we were all glad to get back to the hotel for lunch.

We once more had to use some shelter for the daily line-out session, this time a warehouse across the road from the hotel. Then we again studied a video of our last match against France in Paris before having an early night.

On the Friday we had a stroke of luck in getting hold of a decent scrummaging machine and had a good session. Then the forwards linked up with the backs and the whole team looked sharp, including John Rutherford, which was a great relief. In the afternoon we watched the opening match of the Cup tournament between New

Zealand and Italy. I felt sorry for the Italians who were completely out-classed and who went down 70-6. That night we had the traditional visit to the cinema to see *Platoon*, a pretty gruesome Vietnam film.

The next day I felt that this was the most important date we'd had in Scottish rugby so far. The feeling amongst the Scots camp was that if we beat France in Christchurch we had a chance of going all the way. There was a meeting in Derrick's room to have a last minute discussion. A light lunch of omelette, chips and the now traditional Mars bar. There were telegrams of good wishes from various bodies, including the Scottish Sports Council.

Arriving at the ground we found it in absolutely perfect condition, like a bowling green. The local province, Canterbury, had been having a great run in the Ranfurly Shield and had ploughed their gate money into a £90,000 drainage system. The sun was shining and as we changed in the dressing room we could hear a pipe band playing on the pitch. To hear the pipes so far from home brought a lump to the throat.

I went out to toss a coin with Daniel Dubroca to decide the direction we would play. There was a roar of delight when I came back to tell the boys I'd won the toss and had elected to play with the very low sun at our back. Even before a ball was kicked I felt we would do well. There was a tremendous atmosphere amongst the team.

It was only minutes before we had four points on the board, but to tell you the truth, I'm still puzzled about the way it came about. There was a line-out inside the French half. As I went to throw in I saw we only had two men in the line. Now I'm the only one who can decide when a shortened line-out is required and I hadn't asked for that. No one has admitted calling for it on the Scottish side so it may well have been that a Frenchman called and in the noise the boys took up their position for the two-man line.

Anyway I threw a long one over the tail and Finlay Calder, who had already been in action with a great run, caught the ball, ripped through the French defence and sent out a perfect scoring pass to Derek White. Unfortunately Gavin Hastings missed the conversion although at that stage we didn't know how vital an extra couple of points would have been.

Just after this we had a disaster. Rutherford, who seemed to have completely recovered from his Bermuda injury, had to compete for a high ball from the line-out and in a crushing tackle Sella put him down. That ended John's appearance in the World Cup and after being stretchered off he was soon on his way home to Scotland where fortunately an exploratory operation revealed that the damage wasn't as bad as first feared.

It was a blow. But full marks to Doug Wyllie who moved to stand-off with Alan Tait of Kelso coming in for his first cap in Doug's place at centre. Alan's a strong, very gifted lad whom I thought might make the team anyway on sheer ability.

We got over our shock at losing John and proceeded to take the game to the French again. Our scrummaging was first-class, again mainly due to Iain 'The Bear' Milne, and we took three strikes against the head. In addition those daily line-out sessions were paying dividends and we did well in that department. But it was our tackling which really got to the opposition. We put down everything that moved, without any ceremony. The French were getting rattled, throwing punches in the front row of the scrum and in the rucks. But we took all that and it made us knit closer as a team. By half-time we led 13-6, with Gavin adding three penalty goals to the try, while the French had a couple of penalties.

An advertising break for the great god television meant that the half-time split was five minutes, double the normal time. My team talk to the boys was simple — keep playing this way and keep tackling.

When play resumed the desperate French threw everything at us and eventually from a two-man line in our territory, Berbizier gave to Champ who in turn sent Sella over for an unconverted try. Then Berbizier himself touched down a similar score from a five-metre scrum. However Gavin had landed another penalty so we led 16-14 with ten minutes to go.

Winger Matt Duncan had a nasty head gash caused by a stray French boot, but stayed on. Then disaster struck again for us when Matt, following a typical bull-dozing run, was judged to have failed to release the ball when tackled. It seemed to us that he had not really been held but had somersaulted out of the so-called tackle. Berbizier meantime had rolled off the field to get medical attention while I went up to Matt who was suffering from his head and face injury and looking light-headed. Our physio Dave McLean was standing by to come on and treat him as soon as the referee gave permission. I shouted to the referee to allow Dave on, but evidently he didn't hear me. The next think I knew was a chorus of shouts from our lads and I turned round to see Blanco touching down between the posts. The ball had been lying handy for the penalty to be taken and he had taken advantage to tap it and run while all the medical aid was being administered. What you might call a controversial try.

When we lined up waiting for Blanco's successful conversion kick I had to ask the lads for yet more effort. But I thought, "God knows how they'll produce it. They've given their all."

So there we were with time running out and suddenly down by 20-16. With typical guts the boys refused to give up. It was wee Roy Laidlaw with a deft kick who took play into the French 22. Then Roy fed White who put Matt in at the corner with a beautiful pass — a magical try.

Now it was all down to Gavin who had the chance to win the game with his conversion kick. It was a difficult one, from the touch line and with a ball that neither he nor many of the other kickers were happy about. He struck it well only to see it go off target by about a foot. But he had played magnificently throughout and no one was going to blame him. The referee whistled no side with the scores tied at 20-20.

In the dressing room there was joy and sadness. Joy, particularly for Tait's first cap, and sadness to hear that John was going home. At the official dinner Dubroca, my opposite number and captain, made a nice gesture when he took off his own personal player's tie to give to John. That evening I reflected on how proud I was of the team which had once again run the Five Nations champions off their feet in a pulsating match full of movement and drama. At the back of my mind, though, I now felt certain that because of the tournament ruling regarding tries scored in a drawn match we were fated to meet the All Blacks in two weeks' time.

Chapter 18

PRISON GARB

AT THE official dinner which followed the exciting French game the Tricolours were strangely subdued, although I must say I can hardly remember any Frenchman ever letting his hair down after a match. They went off early after taking no part in the sing-song which started at the Scots table, while we carried on until the early hours with the other guests.

Next morning, it being a Sunday, the "Reverend" Finlay Calder, that prince of jokers, decreed that there should be a Sunday School where a compulsory glass of wine was drunk. Then it was off to the airport bound for Wellington. When we arrived a Scot who had settled there produced a tape recorder which belted out the Corries singing *Flower of Scotland* — a nice gesture and one all the players appreciated. Our hotel was a little to the north of Wellington and when we arrived I phoned Val who told me she was going off with my mum and the boys to Tenerife for a short break. I was glad they were going to have a holiday, however short.

We trained next day at a local ground and although we had a good session for about an hour there were a lot of niggling injury worries. The Bear had a thigh strain, Alan Tomes and Roy Laidlaw had Achilles' tendon trouble, Derek White had a pulled hamstring, Keith Robertson a groin strain, Iain Paxton a calf muscle injury and to top it all I strained my back scrummaging at the end of the training session and I could hardly hobble off the field.

We had some treatment at the hotel then went to see the Wales v Ireland game. I must say I was disappointed in the Irish play but Wales were the better team on the day and deserved their 13-6 win. There was a Government reception at a local club and The Bear and I were kindly asked out to dinner later.

I slept well that night but my back was aching when I woke and I had difficulty in getting up. However I managed to go along to the daily training and put in a bit of light work although I felt bad about not taking a full part. I had more treatment for my back in the afternoon and most of the lads went off golfing or ten-pin bowling which I couldn't face. However I spent a few hours with Roy Laidlaw, The Bear, Greig Oliver and Alan Tait in the hotel jacuzzi and sauna, which cheered me up and also eased the pain in my back. I phoned Val again that night and she and the boys sounded in great spirits. It's good when you phone home and find everyone OK.

I had another early night and on Wednesday, 27 May, we were all up around 8 a.m. for Dave McLean our physio to carry out tests. Dave has been doing this work since 1981/82. What he does is measure a player's fat content to prove that not all rugby men are fat slobs. I found I had put on 2 kilos since leaving home but my fat content was actually down so that the extra weight was made up of muscle. I was pleased about that because when you are on tour there are so many meals that you are pretty well bound to put on weight, so you have to watch what you eat.

We had a bit of a bonus that day for we had so many players on the slightly injured list that training was cancelled. At least it looked like a bonus as we all gathered in the hotel foyer about 10 a.m. We were then driven a few miles out into the hills, dumped at a lay-by and told to walk back to the hotel. I was in a group with Matt Duncan, Iwan Tukalo, Scott Hastings and Richard Cramb who had been touring with Middlesex in Australia and who had joined the squad in place of John Rutherford. At first all went well but then to our horror we found we'd taken a wrong turning and had to trek back to the top of the hill then down to the main road by the route we should have gone in the first place. We were knackered when we got there but city slicker Iwan knew the answer. He bought us cream cakes, rang for a taxi and we landed back at the hotel in style.

That night after dinner we had a meeting at which that forthright character Derrick Grant pointed out to us that we hadn't won a World Cup game yet although everyone was talking already about an All Blacks v Scotland quarter-final. I felt it was about 50 per cent certain that would happen but having watched a video of the Romania v Zimbabwe match which Romania had only won by 21-20 I didn't count on Zimbabwe being pushovers. I noted in my diary: "This is a game we MUST win." There was a sad moment when the boys gathered to wave John Rutherford goodbye as he headed for his plane home.

On the Thursday my back had much improved and I took a full part in a three-hour training session, then had the usual line-out drill, with Jeremy Campbell-Lamerton standing in for the injured Derek White. We had a Maori evening which turned out to be most enjoyable. We were taken a few miles to a meeting house where we had to take off our shoes before entering. Then we touched noses with our hosts who welcomed us in three speeches, with a song after each one. We had to reply in kind and our liaison officer made the first speech, followed by the boys singing *Bonny Mary of Argyll*; then Bob Munro the tour manager did his stuff, followed by *Flower of Scotland*, and finally The Bear spoke exceptionally well and we ended by singing *Will ye go Lassie go?*

That finished the official part of the evening and we went through to another part of the meeting house to sample a Maori meal. This is cooked in a basket on top of red hot stones in a specially dug trench. Cloth is laid over the basket and water poured on to create steam. Then the trench is filled with earth while the meal cooks. It's really a primitive form of pressure cooker but believe me the meal itself was delicious.

The Maoris entertained us after dinner with some of their songs — a moving experience — and gave a demonstration of the Haka which has come to be associated with the All Blacks rugby team and strikes terror into the opposition before the game has started. Some of our boys got up on stage eventually to give a Scottish version of the Haka but I don't think it would have scared even the most junior of All Blacks!

When we got back to the hotel the usual weather temperatures came up on the television screen, with two columns showing the projected temperature for the whole of New Zealand on one side and that for the various cities on the other. There was at most a difference of one or two degrees. This prompted Alex Brewster to say in all seriousness later, "Did you see those rugby scores on the TV? All the games were very close." He's still trying to live that one down.

That night I slept well but the weather was terrible, so much so that we thought the hotel windows would be blown in. It was also sheeting with rain. Next morning we found that Roy wasn't fit enough to play on the Saturday against Zimbabwe so Hawick had its first scrum-half cap lined up in the shape of Greig Oliver. It was quite a coincidence for I was gaining my 50th cap, Greig was Hawick's 50th cap and the first one from the club in his particular position.

Before going to bed I had a chat with Bob Munro and the SRU secretary Bill Hogg. All the players knew Bob well but Bill seemed a bit aloof from them in his ivory tower at Murrayfield. However on tour he became one of the boys and the players took him to their hearts. He trained every day, joined in the sing-songs and had a beer with us. I'm sure that now he knows some of the problems and anxieties of the boys he'll be a great asset to the game in Scotland.

Bill of course was amongst the spectators when, after a 35-minute bus ride, we got to the ground to find the notorious Wellington wind whipping sharply down the pitch. When the team photo was taken I asked Greig and Alan Tait, who was on his first full match, to sit on either side of me in order to give them a bit of a lift. I went out on to the pitch with Derrick and Ian McGeechan and decided that I'd play with the wind behind our backs if I was lucky enough to win the toss. However Malcolm Jellicoe, the Zimbabwe skipper, guessed correctly. Imagine our surprise and delight to find, when we took the field, that he had elected to play against the wind.

My plan was to get points on the board and tighten up our game in the second-half to counteract the wind. It all went like a dream early on and within five minutes Alan Tait was over for his first try. I'm glad to say that Oliver too got a try on his debut — a big thrill for him and all of Hawick — and in all we crossed the Zimbabwean line 11 times. Our tries came from Tait, Paxton, Duncan, Tukalo who each had two, Oliver, Jeffrey and Hastings who had one apiece. In addition Gavin Hastings had eight conversions. We had led 40-6 at the interval but Zimbabwe had to come back some time and to their credit they scored a good try through Dick Budentag, while Grobler goaled five penalties and a conversion. To us it had been unknown territory and I was glad the game was out of the way.

Following the usual after match interviews and my thanks to the

Zimbabwean boys, I returned to the Scots dressing room to thank my own troops. I found the boys had clubbed together and bought me a gold salver and four goblets to mark my 50th cap. Evidently Roy had made a tear-jerking speech only to find at the end of it I was still being interviewed outside the dressing room and knew nothing about it. So Roy made another speech which Finlay Calder told me wasn't a patch on the first — how I wish I had been there. But I was tremendously touched. It's a great honour to play for your country, but to be honoured by your fellow international players must be the supreme accolade. Back at the hotel the celebrations went on to an early hour with the Zimbabwean boys joining in. It's not every day you get a 50th cap and not every day you get a 50th international from a club.

Next day, Sunday, 31 May, I was duty boy along with Jeremy Campbell-Lamerton. You don't get any preferential treatment on tour even if you are captain. We had an early light training session then took the plane to Dunedin, changing at Christchurch. There was a delay of half an hour and it was my job to get sandwiches and drinks for the boys. Have you ever tried getting 30 rounds of sandwiches and coffee in a wee cafe? Not to be recommended. However we got to Dunedin eventually and we were soon watching a video of Scotland v Romania just to get our minds on to Romania and their style of play.

On Monday, 1 June, we had a training session which lasted about 90 minutes but was nothing too strenuous. However The Bear left the field early with a calf strain, as did Finlay Calder who had a shin injury. Full-back Gavin Hastings had strained his back and took no part but Roy Laidlaw was active again.

The boys decided to stay in the hotel that evening and watch a video film. I was just about to join them when Doug Smith, our President, Bill Connon, the Vice-President, and Ken Smith, a member of the International Board, asked me to join them for a drink at their dinner table. I didn't have a drink but we had an informal two-hour discussion which I greatly enjoyed and I hope they did. We talked about what might follow on from the World Cup and I put the case for the players to have more say in decisions, obviously those of the SRU in particular, and the need for more communication between us. Hopefully that will come about soon now the first World Cup is over.

Next day we were up early to meet the Romanian challenge.

Because the kick-off had been advanced to 1 p.m. our preliminary talk in the hotel before leaving was at 9.30 a.m. Coach Grant emphasised how vital the game was as we were in a knockout situation and must beat Romania to get a quarter-final place. It was a short bus journey from our hotel to the Carisbrook ground which was in magnificent nick, certainly in stark contrast to my last visit in 1983 when it was covered with two or three inches of rain which helicopters tried to clear.

I wanted to play with the wind but Romania won the toss. Again, though, as against Zimbabwe we were lucky, for they elected to play against the wind and sun in the first-half. We had dedicated this match to Norrie Rowan who had come in for the injured Milne. Norrie was pretty well a professional dirt tracker — that's a player who backs up the top boy. But he's a tremendously good prop and we were all delighted to have him in the side. Apart from getting the Romanians to do what we had wanted, we had to kick-off as well. Our forwards were lined up on the left of the field, but Gavin Hastings put in a neat little chip to the right, Matt Duncan gathered and raced away. The ball went through several Scots hands and came back to Matt who dived over the line for what could have been the quickest ever try in international rugby. However referee Steve Hilditch decided that there had been a forward pass somewhere along the way. I didn't think so . . . I thought the referee, like the Romanians, had been caught napping by Gavin's kick-off.

On top of having the score chalked off poor Scott Hastings, in for his first World Cup game, pulled up with a hamstring injury that had kept him out of the previous matches and was helped off with his World Cup career lasting about 20 seconds. A real blow but Cramb came on, Doug Wyllie moved back to centre from stand-off, and we were in business again. So much so that we built up a 33-7 lead by the interval and went on to win by 55-28. Gavin Hastings set up a new world record when he scored 27 points from two tries, eight conversions and a penalty goal . . . but it only lasted a couple of hours as Didier Camberabero notched up 30 points for France in their 70-12 win over Zimbabwe. More important than records to us at this stage was the fact that apart from the loss of Scott we also lost two of our best forwards, Alan Tomes, who had to leave with a shoulder injury, and John Jeffrey, the flanker, who scored three tries then went off with an ankle injury, a blow to the chest and a cut head. We played the last quarter with only 14 men but still remained in the driving seat. Our tempo had slowed down in the second-half but I put that down to the usual long five-minute half-time break they have in New Zealand when the boys started thinking about their next task, the quarter-final against the All Blacks.

Next day we had an early start to catch the flight to Christchurch. Because we had been playing in two internationals within four days there was no training and we were glad just to laze around the hotel, have a couple of beers in a nearby pub and get to bed early.

I was awake early on Thursday, 4 June, for a New Zealand radio station was on the phone at 7 a.m. It had been running a competition about making your dream come true and the winner was a Hawick lady who wanted to speak to me and Bill McLaren. So after speaking to her on the phone I didn't really get to sleep again. Anyway the forwards had a 9 a.m. scrummaging session before we picked up the backs at 10 a.m., then off we all went to Paparua prison where I'm sure they must have a cell reserved for the Scottish team. The Bear was still feeling his calf muscle injury a bit and I hoped he'd be OK for the final training session next day. One or two of the boys turned their ankles on the stony ground but there didn't seem to be anything serious.

Before we left, the prison governor presented me with a New Zealand prison officer's hat to mark the fact that on the Saturday I'd be equalling the Scottish record, held by my old mate Jim Renwick, of 52 caps. The boys insisted I wear it all the way back on the bus but it was a gesture I appreciated from the prison authorities. That night we watched a couple of videos of New Zealand playing France and then their latest game against the Argentine to familiarise ourselves with their likely tactics. After that I dashed upstairs to phone Val. She sounded a bit harassed because she'd just come home from Tenerife but it was good to know everyone at home was fine. While I was on the line the operator chipped in to say there was a call from Scotland so I said my goodbyes. The caller was Radio Tweed, our local Border station who wanted an interview. Then they linked me up with John Rutherford. It was good to hear from him and better still that he should confirm he'd be back playing next season.

On the Friday night we put our final plans into effect. Everything went well in a one-hour session. The boys were razor-sharp and all we did went with the precision of a well-honed machine. Then Bill McLaren and I met the competition winner, Kathleen Wallace, who had been a fellow pupil at Trinity Primary with me, and also her husband and mum and dad. After that there were interviews with the New Zealand Press boys who thought we'd do well the next day. We got back to the hotel to find good luck telegrams from a variety of people willing us to win, including one from the Lord Provost of Edinburgh. I got a congratulations card for Derek 'Styx' Turnbull who was going in against the All Blacks for his first cap next day — what a baptism! — in place of John Jeffrey who was still on the injured list. So 'Styx' became the 51st Hawick player to be capped and it was a well-deserved honour.

The senior players met Derrick and Ian McGeechan to work out our tactics. They were simple — to scrum well, deny them good line-out ball and keep the ball in front of the forwards. In other words to play New Zealand at their own uncomplicated type of game. My last thought that night before I dropped off to sleep was, "God, how I hope we win tomorrow."

As all the world now knows, it was not to be.

Chapter 19

BORDER RUGBY

IN THE part of the world where I have played my club rugby we have a unique set-up known as the Border League. I can assure you it's just as hard and competitive as the national league which brings with it the title of national champions. As Hawick over the past few seasons have been the national champions, or at worst runners-up, the team is always the target for the rest of the Border clubs who make up the Border League.

One of our toughest assignments is to go to Milntown to play Langholm. The club is always struggling for players but they are always robust and fight every inch of the way. I'm truly sorry that they have now gone down to Division III, but I'm certain that their tenacity and will to win must see them back competing at the top once more in seasons to come. I well remember my first baptism of fire at Milntown when I was a raw young lad. A well-kent figure, Hector Barnfather, who is certainly no respector of persons, was at flanker. At the first scrum suddenly everything went blank. I couldn't see a thing. Only after I had scrubbed away at my eyes did I see the cause . . . it was Hector throwing handfuls of mud in my face!

The Langholm supporters are partisan to say the least. They move up and down the touch-line and it gets a bit depressing to see the same faces when you line up for a throw-in. But they do support the side and their loyalty deserves reward.

Langholm and Selkirk are the nearest clubs to us in the Border set-up. On their day and at full strength Selkirk are as good as any side in the country. Their problem is that they don't have reserves in depth to take over from key players like their Lions No.8 Iain Paxton, the brilliant stand-off John Rutherford, international scrum-half Gordon Hunter and international winger Iwan Tukalo. All of these players have been hit by injury over the past two or three seasons and, deprived of ball possession, Selkirk have often had to struggle because of this. The townsfolk and team at Selkirk are known as Souters, which stems from a shoe-making tradition but they are also called Japs because, I'm led to believe, the town is built on a hill similar to one in Tokyo!

Of all the teams we meet in our area the one which really gets the old adrenalin flowing is Gala. Rivalry between us seems to be bred in the bone.

They have been going through a sticky patch of late and I'm sorry — although that may seem strange coming from a Hawick man — to see them temporarily in Division II. No matter, our game against them in the Border League will be just as fiercely contested as ever. I'm not the first Hawick captain to have told my team that for many of them playing against Gala is the nearest thing they'll get to playing in a Scotland jersey. Despite the rivalry I'm glad to say I have friends in the Gala camp like Peter Dods and Gordon Dickson. I turned down the chance to play in a Hawick Seven once so I could attend Gordon's wedding, and greater love hath no Hawick man than that!

One team we find very difficult to beat on their lovely home ground, at the Greenyards, is Melrose. Our final game with them is usually a midweek one near the end of the season. In fact, that happens so often that I have a feeling the Border League secretary must have Melrose affiliations.

In the past Melrose have gloried in such names as their famous half-back partnership Dave Chisholm and Eck Hastie who went together like bacon and eggs or strawberries and cream. They have had mixed fortunes lately, but they always seem to produce the goods when the chips are down. They have fine forwards currently in George Runciman and the McLeish brothers, a neat little stand-off in David Sheil and of course their international winger or centre, the elusive Keith Robertson. No one can follow Keith once he starts on a mazy run, you can only run straight up-field and hope somehow to link up with him. But he can side-step on a sixpence, has a searing burst of pace to take him past the opposition and on his day is simply world-class.

In season 1987/88 Jim Telfer is taking over as club coach — he's an old Melrose player — so I expect big things from the Greenyards apart from their famous seven-a-side tournament which must be the best organised in the world.

You can't say the name Jed-forest rugby club without conjuring up a picture of their famous scrum-half, Roy Laidlaw. What a servant he has been to them. To see this little man of 12 stones hurling himself at guys twice his size, going down and then getting up with a shake to return to the fray is really something. I would recommend all aspiring young players to try and copy Roy's dedication and sense of duty to his side.

It's true that, like Gala, Jed will be appearing in Division II in season 1987/88. That's despite the fact that they actually beat us at their picturesiue ground at Riverside. Jed's trouble has been inconsistency. One week they play like the national champions, the next they slide to defeat when least expected. But they can take heart from the up-and-coming players they have nurtured like Harry Hogg and Gary Armstrong. As for Roy I know he'll continue to help Jed out at every chance. Of all the friends Val and I have made in rugby I rate our relationship with Roy and his wife Joy as No.1. A great guy who is a credit to a great wee club.

Kelso, for my money, will continue to be the team which we in Hawick must regard as the most dangerous threat to our national title. They have for a long time had a vastly experienced back division including Roger Baird, Andrew Ker and Bob Hogarth. In recent seasons my highly regarded hooker understudy, Gary Callander, has got the forwards on song. Fellows like John 'White Shark' Jeffrey and the toothless tiger Eric Paxton spell real danger to any opposing pack. Kelso, to my mind, are the most clear-thinking team we've had to compete against in the last few seasons. They study the way we play and then attack our weak spots. I know we'll have to keep a wary eye in coming seasons if we are to deny them their ultimate aim of taking the national title as well as the Border League crown.

Every team in the Border set-up produces their best play when they meet us. The Border League is played on a home and away basis which means 12 matches, and the national league takes up

Ewan Common tries to stop me — and did, I think. (Courtesy: Ian Brand)

another 13 Saturdays. So you can realise we haven't much time for 'friendlies' and when we do play them it's always against top sides like Gosforth, Headingley or Heriot's. The result is that Hawick go into action every week as fit if not fitter than any other club in the country and always knowing that the opposition would love to shoot us down.

One of the national league teams who cause us a lot of problems is West of Scotland. On their day they can produce the same kind of forward power that we rely on. Indeed, I remember a few years back being cleaned out in the hooking business by that wily old bird Quintin Dunlop, ably assisted by guys like Sandy Carmichael, Gordon Brown and David Gray, with of course my old friend and current work colleague, prop Gerry McGuinness.

The only other club who really posed any problems to us from the West side of the country was Jordanhill, now sadly out of the premier division. But in their heyday, with guys like 43 times capped Ian McLauchlan and Richie Dixon in their ranks, with the team coached by Bill Dickinson who was the first man to become the Scotland coach, they always gave us a hard, bruising battle. I have one vivid memory of their Kilmardinny pitch. I had kicked ahead, a little too strongly, but was following up and in my eagerness made a frantic dive to touch the ball down. Unknown to me there was a burn just behind the dead ball line and I finished up soaking wet and had to play the remainder of the game with the water dripping off me. At least I had the satisfaction of scoring at the other end after the interval.

· Moving over to the East and particularly Edinburgh, there is a wealth of talented clubs, none more so than Heriot's. We usually play them three times in a season, once in September, on New Year's Day and of course in the national league. The September game is classed as a friendly, but rarely is. The rivalry between the clubs is almost equivalent to Hawick playing Gala. I think both sides look on this early match as a curtain raiser to the league season and go all out to get the psychological victory.

There's little love between us on the field of play and that's not only because, on my first game at Goldenacre, I was listed in the programme as C. Beans, while Norman Pender was down as N. Bender. Our New Year's Day encounter is something special. It's not regarded as just a fun game and Hogmanay for the Hawick players at least is a very sober affair indeed. It's not the first time I've brought in the New Year with a cup of coffee . . . but at least you've no hangover the next day. When we play Heriot's at Mansfield Park my routine is to take Val and the boys to my mother's home, wish her a Happy New Year, then toddle down to the ground. There's always a special atmosphere and whether it's because of the time of the year, the match is always played in a great spirit.

There's a bit of Hawick rugby folklore about one particular New Year's Day game when the late Cecil Froud, father of Terence who coached the Hawick PSA to the 1986/87 Royal Bank Youth League Final when they beat Howe of Fife, was due to play. However there had been a sharp overnight frost and in the morning the match was declared off. So Cecil naturally went to the nearby pub and was bringing in the New Year in good style when it was revealed that Heriot's had arrived, there had been a bit of a thaw and the game was on. Cecil played and, I'm told, scored two great tries, which perhaps is a sign that a couple of pints before a match can make you relaxed enough to play without any inhibition.

Since the official national league championship began Heriot's and Gala are the only two teams apart from Hawick to take the title. That's why we regard our national championship match with the Goldenacre side as being so important and why they always raise their game against us. I have had the doubtful privilege over the years of playing against my Scotland right arm Iain Milne and his brothers David and Kenny, forming a front row known affectionately as the Three Bears. Heriot's usually field a tigerish back row as well and they still call on the services when things are going wrong for them of that great scrum-half Alan Lawson and the incomparable full-back Andy Irvine.

Boroughmuir is another Edinburgh side which has posed us problems, although I for one am grateful to them for their knack of beating teams who are snapping at Hawick heels. The players over the years have included many good friends, such as Bill Watson, Bruce Hay, Norrie Rowan and Bob Cunningham.

Our match in season 1986/87 was a vital one for us. Hawick could field only three forward regulars — Jock Rae, Derek Turnbull and myself. So we were given no chance against Boroughmuir, especially as the game was on their pitch at Meggatland. But our five alleged substitutes played out of their skins and we romped home winners by 28-19 in a match where I had the satisfaction of scoring a try. At a squad session next day preparing for an international, the Kelso forward John Jeffrey sought me out to say that after that win Hawick deserved to take the national title for the tenth time. I appreciated that coming from John, for his club were obviously hoping that we would go down to 'Muir and pave the way for them to take the title for the first time.

Another Edinburgh team who always give us a run for our money is Watsonians. Their only drawback is that, being a closed side, they usually have to get by with young, inexperienced forwards. But they certainly make the most of their assets. And of course with backs like Gavin and Scott Hastings, Euan Kennedy, Stuart Johnston and Gordon Forbes, they're always menacing when they get the ball and run. With the Calder boys, John, Jim and Finlay in their pack the Stewart's/Melville team are also a team which need watching.

All in all, I think the official league which started in a hopeful rather than certain fashion back in season 1973/74 has proved its

A proud moment with Hawick: L-R Ken Smith, C. Deans, Bill Millar. Scottish Championship and Border League 1984-85 season.

worth. Every game is competitive and the championship is worthy of the whole Scottish rugby set-up. It used to be the case that only Hawick, Gala and Heriot's were looked upon as having any chance of taking the title. But the competition gets fiercer every season and you can't rule out teams like Kelso, Selkirk or West of Scotland aiming for the top. The competitive build-up, I'm sure, led to our Grand Slam triumph of 1984 and the benefit is felt not only by the Scotland squad but by the B team and the Under-21s, whose players have had experience of first division rugby.

I count myself very lucky indeed to have been a member of one of the greatest clubs ever to grace Scottish rugby. Hawick's scalp is one that every other club longs to take. Fortunately, that doesn't happen often, especially at Mansfield Park, although full marks to Kelso who brought off a win there on 13 April 1987. I think that was our first loss at home since September 1985.

With the Border League set-up plus the national championship every game played must be taken seriously. I am just thankful to have been with a side like Hawick which has always been in the top bracket of Scottish rugby over the years.

Chapter 20

WORLD RUGBY — THE FUTURE

NOW that the World Cup is over the legislators of the International Board must get together to wipe out the anomalies that threaten rugby as we know it. There is so much sponsorship money floating about that realistically some kind of professional or semi-professional sport could replace, in five or six years, our so-called amateur game and that would be a tremendous pity.

Personally I'm privileged to work with a firm which pays my salary when I'm away on tour or training. But why, I ask myself, should someone suffer financially to help draw crowds of millions all over the world? Why should any international rugby player have to lose a weekly wage whilst travelling thousands of miles to represent his country, knowing his firm can't afford his wages unless he's actually there? I personally can't understand this system.

At the same time some of our fellow players are obviously doing well. It was disturbing during the World Cup to see top New Zealand stars appearing on TV advertising everything from farm machinery to rub ointments. I know our forthright President, Dr Doug Smith, was as perturbed as myself and the Scots squad. I know also we Scots have the reputation of being the "squares" of world rugby. In the past we've always sought to play the game by the spirit and not just the letter of the laws. But how can you reconcile the blatant advertising we saw in New Zealand with the fact that a guy like John Rutherford of Selkirk was forbidden to accept in public his richly deserved *Rugby World* Player of the Year Award because the SRU maintain that rugby is a team game and individuals should not be singled out for honours?

It reminds me of the days before the official league championships came into being. Newspaper correspondents had to work out the points and percentages and come up with the winning team. That was, of course, ignored by the SRU but at dinners and other social events the winning team would generously be referred to as champions.

During the World Cup I got a call from a New Zealand newspaper saying an article by a good journalist friend of mine, Peter Bills, had appeared in a Sunday paper. He had quoted me criticising the All Blacks for advertising. But I was merely speaking for the rest of the Scots squad as well as myself. I've also been quoted as saying that if they didn't stop we'd start. I'm certainly not keen for that to happen but it would be a natural development if the present state of affairs is allowed to continue.

I got the impression that the men at the top didn't want to create waves while the first World Cup was taking place. Fair enough. But they must get down to tackling this problem now that it is over. After all, the game is supposed to be for players all over the world. If the International Board won't take the responsibility to lay down the law for everyone it'll be a sad day and I've no doubt that the emerging rugby nations will, without a strong lead, take matters into their own hands.

On the subject of any future World Cup there must be a case for South Africa to be included. I'm talking purely as a player and not a politican and I know that idea will go down like a ton of bricks on a glasshouse in many quarters. People keep saying you can't separate sport from politics, conveniently forgetting it was the politicians who infiltrated sport for their own ends. Hitler started it when trying to put over his Aryan supermen until Jesse Owens upset his plan. Since then however the politicians, never a breed to dispense with any bad idea, have interfered at all levels from the Olympics down.

I've been invited several times to go to South Africa to play in either 15-a-side rugby or sevens tournaments. I've never been able to accept because of commitments back home. But, yes, I'd really love to go there and play. I think it's about the only rugby-playing country I've never visited. Some of my club-mates like Jim Renwick and Alan Tomes who have been there have told me about the great playing conditions.

There have been rumours of course that players touring over there recently have been paid to do so. If that is the case then it's a shame the Republic has to resort to that to get games with other countries. With the World Cup having taken place without South Africa competing I fear the authorities might have dug a grave for themselves. It could lead to exactly the professional or semi-professional tours that they most fear. South Africa is undoubtedly a great place in which to play rugby. It will be a shame if they cannot get teams over to provide the competition required to play the sport at world class. If and when they get their country sorted out it might mean having to start from scratch, although they still have some fantastic players around.

I've played alongside South Africans over here and I must say I've always found them perfect gentlemen. In particular I've struck up a special relationship with Rob Louw who now plays Rugby League for Wigan. Rob and I have exchanged jerseys and we're good buddies. Rob has invited me down to Wigan more than once and when I do decide to hang up my boots I think I'll take him up on his offer and go down to see some Rugby League.

I must say I like watching Rugby League nowadays. About ten years ago in Britain it wasn't much cop. But since the Australians started touring over here and a lot of them have now settled with British clubs — sometimes I think there are more Australians playing in Britain than in Australia — it's a different ball game. The Australians have brought a whole new dimension to the sport and I'm convinced the success of the Australian amateur rugby team owes a lot to Australian Rugby League. The players seem to have played the game in their school days. Certainly they have mastered the art of making the ball available all the time so that if they are tackled their passes are quickly away to the support. I watched a lot of Rugby League when we toured in Australia and was very impressed.

In fact, when I was a teenager of 17 or 18 I was under scrutiny by Salford Rugby League Club. One of their local scouts in Hawick, Jimmy Chalmers, had tipped them off and I believe some of their committee came up to have a look at me. But I didn't get any firm offer and in those days I wouldn't have considered turning pro. Now

213

the game is more expansive and it might be a different kettle of fish but I really can't see me as a league player.

Rugby League can be pretty tough — but so too can Rugby Union. Dirty play has always been a worry to me because of the position in the middle of the front row in which I play. But believe you me, even if I could turn the clock back I'd never want to play in any other place.

Under the old rules there was always the possibility of a serious neck injury when the scrum collapsed. Or you got some maniac coming through from the second row and kicking you in the head. Mind you, some people take the view that if a front row forward does get kicked in the head it won't make any difference to him!

I was pretty scared in my very first game against England when their pack shunted us back at a fair rate of knots and the scrum collapsed on several occasions, possibly intentionally on our part to stop ourselves being pushed over the line, and I got kicked in the head a few times. That could have meant an early finish to my career. However I survived and accepted it as a normal progression through the internationl scene.

You learn fast but there are times in scrummages when I've literally had my eyes closed and hoped a second-row offender would miss when a punch seemed on the cards. For, with my arms round each of my props, there's no way I can defend myself. One ploy which used to bother me a lot was when a tight head prop would have his head band treated with some kind of liniment. When the front rows locked antlers he would bore in and the rub would sting like hell as you felt your eyes burning.

The position with regard to scrum dangers has been helped by the present rule whereby a prop's shoulders cannot be below his hips. This lessens considerably the dangers of scrums collapsing and possible neck injuries. But it's still a physical, aggressive, demanding sort of game and I've had the odd cut which needed stitching. Val reckons I've got a thick skin but I don't know if she means that as a compliment!

One of the most brutal things I've witnessed was in the Grand Slam game against France at Murrayfield. My old pal Iain 'The Bear' Milne was simply cleaning up the French scrum with some awesome power. The French couldn't keep on taking the pressure and decided to take things into their own hands. Poor Iain was repeatedly punched in every scrum. But he just absorbed it all and kept on getting more and more power into his scrummaging until you could actually feel the French forwards buckling and finally throwing in the towel.

The only other country I've found who will use physical aggression to the full is New Zealand where ripped skins and lingering scars are worn like discreet medals beneath the shirts of the front row men. Find one unscarred and you find a player shirking his responsibilities. A hooker is only as good as the protection which is provided by the props.

In New Zealand the law of the jungle triumphs. A player not releasing the ball is unceremoniously rucked out from the scrum. In Britain that would be illegal play. Not in my eyes, for players would not hang around clutching the ball if they knew they were liable to be rucked away from the base of the scrum. We could learn a lot from New Zealand in that respect.

Overall, international rugby is a hard enough, and a physically demanding enough, sport without having to worry about dirty play. I'm glad to say the home unions are now helping by not selecting dirty players. After the Wales v England game this season I was glad to see England ban players because of their behaviour on the pitch. But my theory is that it takes two to fight and Wales should also have held an inquiry into this match.

Rugby is a game where a straight punch or a wild boot could cripple or even kill a person and that does worry me at times. But if you did sit down and think what could happen in your life you wouldn't go out of the house, let alone play a physical sport like rugby. 99.9 per cent of men playing the game know what could happen. It is the .1 per cent I think should leave the game — or the administrators should act to make them leave.

It's mainly because of that tiny minority of dirty players that we need no-nonsense referees. In Scotland I reckon we have, overall, a pretty good standard of whistlers. I think two of the best we've had in recent years have been Allan Hosie, now retired, and Brian Anderson. Anderson is on the international panel and I think he should get more games to handle, for he's very good indeed. Both he and Hosie have been the type of referee who wouldn't penalise you unless it was necessary. I also liked Norman Sanson who was unfairly treated after sending two players off in an international. I am not too sure about some other top Scottish referees but, as I say, overall we're pretty lucky.

English referees belong to THE Rugby Union and don't hesitate to let you know that. Roger Quittenton used to be always, to my mind, playing to the crowd but he has quietened down a bit now, although he still wants to be part of the action. I think Laurie Prideaux is more a player's referee. However the English top men are pretty fair.

Moving on to Wales, the first figure that springs to mind is the huge Clive Norling. The game is bigger than he is but he doesn't appear to know that. He's always wanting to be the centre of attraction — an arrogant referee. I rather liked Derek Bevan who handled the Spanish game in April of 1987. On the whole the Welsh lads are really pretty good although they are inclined to let squint put-ins go unpunished.

Ireland have a well-deserved reputation for good referees. One of my favourites is John West, although Dave Burnett is also very competent. Irish referees handle matches like the Scots, just as the players tend to play similar types of rugby, and they let the game flow.

Talking about allowing the game to flow there's no one better at that than the French. They let minor infringements go but stamp on anything major. It's always good to have a Frenchman in charge, they just let you get on with the game. The only snag is that it can become a bit loose. I liked René Hourquet and of course there was Francis Palmade who, despite refereeing countless games involving English-speaking teams, never managed to speak a word of the language — or so he said.

The only other referees I'll mention are New Zealanders. I thought Keith Lawrence handled Scotland's recent Paris game against France like a veteran although it was his first big occasion. He's a small, bouncy man, very fit and must be one of the best referee exports ever from New Zealand. Then we had Bob Francis the previous season who was also very good. If it came to choice of referees outside Scotland I'd put New Zealand first, because we play the same type of game as they are used to from the All Blacks, French referees second, Irish third and a toss-up between Welsh and English for fourth.

On the international front again, there has been a lot of argument over the years about what song should be sung and played at international matches as a purely Scottish anthem. The players adopted *Flower of Scotland* way back and much prefer that to *Scotland the Brave*, which has up until now been favoured by the SRU. Indeed not so long ago the Scottish players were each handed song sheets of *Scotland the Brave* so that we would know the words! We promptly tore them up and when we did get on the pitch sang our usual *Flower of Scotland*. On the way back from New Zealand I had a long chat on that subject with the next President Bill Connon and I hope that there will now be a change of heart. It may seem a small thing but it would be appreciated by the guys at the sharp end of the game.

Let's look at the way things are in the rugby world and how they are likely to progress. I see kids being pushed harder and harder, usually by ambitious dads. In our sport in Hawick we don't have any mini or midi rugby. I think it's early enough for a kid of eight, nine or even ten to be introduced to the game. But I see mums and dads shouting and screaming at bairns of five, six or seven from the touch line. All the youngsters want to do is pick up a ball and run. Tackling isn't for them, scrummaging isn't for them. But you get some dad who maybe played for the fifth XV trying to impress on a youngster he must grow up to play for Scotland if not captain them.

I think there's far too much competition for youngsters under ten years old. It's time enough to start competing when you're 12 or 13. Some of these youngsters will have been playing rugby for around 15 years by the time they're 21. Some might stay on but a lot will get tired or blow up and pack in very early. I think the mums and dads have got a lot to answer for when they start pushing their offspring too early. I myself didn't play until I was nine and I was never pushed into it by either my mum or my dad. But I've thoroughly enjoyed the game and still do.

What I've thought of doing, once I get any time, is to get just a couple of the Hawick lads, collect as many youngsters as want to come and take them up to the park. Then I'd let them run with the ball. Forget about forward passes, tackling and scrummaging — just let them enjoy themselves. Kids of that age don't want to be knocked down by other boys who might be bigger than them or risk getting hurt in a scrum. All they want is some fun.

Turning to the two biggest events in Scottish rugby in recent years, the 1984 Grand Slam and the 1987 World Cup, I think we will see the benefits from these coming within the next decade. I hope we don't have to wait ten years for another Slam. But it's rather like everyone plays tennis after Wimbledon, the lads dig out their dad's old golf clubs after the Open, all the boys are kicking footballs after the Cup Final. The benefits of the Slam will be perhaps more gradual but they should be enduring.

One thing which has been worrying rugby enthusiasts like myself has been the dramatic drop in older schoolboys getting the chance to play the game following the recent teachers' industrial action which effectively ended out-of-hours coaching by keen teachers. In 1985 there were about 14,500 schoolboys playing. The following year that number had dropped to just over 4,000. The SRU have been so concerned that they have set up a Youth Marketing Sub-Committee under Fred McLeod to encourage boys to take up the sport. They have scored considerable success already by distributing a World Cup poster, but the best news is that there are indications that schools are taking up rugby once more — about 70 to 80 per cent are now back in the fold. Without these young recruits rugby would soon be in a parlous state.

So far as the current rugby set-up for senior players is concerned, I feel that too many demands are made on them, particularly those with families. There are so many tours, squad sessions and international commitments that the game now really isn't suitable for a married man with youngsters growing up. I'm very fortunate in having an understanding wife and understanding kids. I'm also lucky in the fact that my company have been so tolerant about my rugby playing. But there's no doubt the boys must think what's wrong that their dad isn't at home as much as the dad down the street or across the road. I think there's a strong case for cutting drastically the demands on players.

I'm sure it's a matter that must cause the SRU to think deeply and may I say a few words about the changing attitude of the Scottish Rugby Union? I mean that in no forelock-tugging way. But there is no doubt things have improved tremendously since I first started playing international rugby.

As an example, when Val first came to Edinburgh to see me play in an international and stayed on for the night, there was a dinner for the wives of the committee which was free. Players' wives and girlfriends, on the other hand, either paid for their own meals or went hungry. And if any of the boys who weren't married invited their fiancées or girlfriends along to the after-dinner dance then they had to pay for their rooms. Thank goodness all that privileged, old school tie image has gone now.

Sure, we still have the odd bit of hassle. Recently I was at a Friday session where the Press are always invited to take pictures and have interviews. At the moment the national squad are sponsored by Umbro and wear their goods. Now, the forwards had to do some scrummaging on the machine at this particular time. We knew we were more than likely to tear our Umbro tops if we kept them on for that scrummaging exercise. So the front row boys took their tops off. Unfortunately for me I was wearing an Adidas training jersey underneath and one or two photographs appeared in the newspapers next morning.

We won our game and everyone was in the dressing-room quite delighted when Bob Munro, the manager of this year's World Cup team, came in looking as worried as if we'd lost by 40 points. "Colin," he said, "you've made my life hell." When I gawped at him he explained that Umbro, whose boss is a personal friend of mine, had spotted that I was supporting the rival firm in the Press pictures. I assured everyone that the incident was quite unintentional and one good thing came out of it — all the boys were kitted out with Umbro training jerseys so the same thing wouldn't happen again.

As a player and a Scot, however, I think the SRU nowadays is the best rugby ruling body in the world. They are, I think, the only Union which makes a point of getting in a tour every year. This to my mind is vitally important for the building up of morale, camaraderie and consistency. All these things have helped to improve our play in the past few seasons.

One thing I must say I don't agree with, though, is the Union's policy, stated before the World Cup began, that they are against making any payments to players or their families when long tours are on the agenda. I think it only fair that the normal take-home pay of someone on a tour who requires it should be sent to his wife to keep her free from financial anxiety and to set the player's mind at rest so that he can concentrate on the game.

One other point for the attention of the SRU. When a player is first picked to play for Scotland I think it would be a good idea for whoever it is to get an individual officially typed letter telling him of his selection. That's instead of the current standard photocopy. After all, one of the major achievements, indeed THE major achievement of any Scottish player, is to be selected for his country. A letter of the type I've described would be cherished for life. It's the kind of thing a bloke could show his grandchildren with pride. If my idea is adopted it would cost nothing but a bit of official paper and typist's time, and think what goodwill it would generate. I leave the thought with the SRU selection committee.

I have thankfully received my fair share of these photocopied letters which have brought me 52 caps for my country. Now, at the end of my playing career, I have written this book for what I believe to be the best interests of the game in which I hope to continue in some capacity. Rugby has given me a wonderful life. Now is the time I would like to put something back into the game, in whichever way the authorities will allow me.

Appendix

A Rugby Wife's Tale

by Val Deans

MY greatest dread, one I'm sure shared by thousands of rugby wives, is for the telephone to ring to say my Colin has been seriously injured in a game away from home. When I see rough play I get pretty scared. Thankfully, Colin has not had too many injuries which I think is due in the main to his insistence on fitness before he takes the field. But there is no doubt that this engrained fear is one of the drawbacks to being a player's wife.

There are, however, many compensations. Without being married to a top player I would never have had the thrill of meeting Her Majesty The Queen at Holyroodhouse after the Grand Slam triumph, never have been invited to lunch at Floors Castle when the Duke and Duchess of Roxburgh had the Duchess of Kent as a guest and never have had a meal with the Princess Royal before the start of the 1987 Scotland v Wales game. These were all red letter days and stick in your memory, but to my mind equally as important and more enduring are the friendships struck up by the rugby wives with each other, especially when their husbands are away touring for a lengthy period as during the 1987 World Cup or a British Lions tour.

Probably my best pal is Joy Laidlaw, wife of Roy, the Scotland scrum-half who of course is a great buddy of Colin. Joy and I seem to think on the same wavelength, maybe because we each have two boys, and when I'm feeling a bit low I only have to pick up the phone to hear her cheery voice and I feel better immediately. Relations and neighbours can also give a great deal of support as everyone near me does when Colin is away.

YOU'RE A HOOKER, THEN

In a Scottish captain's house like ours, although it is an amateur game, rugby rules. I can only remember one hurried weekend in season 1986/87 when we had Colin to ourselves. Most of his time for years has been taken up by training, squad sessions, international matches and finally the World Cup tour which meant so much to him and all the Scots boys. I was so pleased and proud for Colin when he led out Scotland against the All Blacks to gain his 52nd record-equalling cap. It seemed a long time since the first one when he had come down to my work to tell me the news, bubbling over with excitement. But every honour for your country is something special and I still got a feeling of emotion each time a letter arrived from the SRU to say he had been selected for yet another game.

Certainly Colin has come a long way since the first time we went out on a blind date, when he still had a bit of puppy fat but already possessed that wonderful grin of his too. My father was a very strict parent and I dreaded it when he asked who I was going out with. When I said Colin Deans however, his face lit up when he realised that Peter Deans, who had played for Hawick, was Colin's dad. "A good rugby family," pronounced my dad. So Colin was taken into my family with open arms. He and my dad, who also had played rugby, chatted away like a couple of gossiping wives about the game.

Talking of gossip, an awful lot of women and girls are suspicious of rugby men and their booze-ups. But the game and a few beers seem to go hand in hand. If you indulge too much you won't get far in such a hard sport. The boys like to relax and unwind in the bar after a game and it's not a bad thing to let your hair down. It's when it happens too often that the women start getting fed up and annoyed. I feel there's a happy medium which has to be followed and mostly is.

Then, of course, there are the women who will raise the question of groupies who are impressed by the sheer physical fitness of the players and who latch on to them during long tours particularly. Hand on heart, I've never heard or seen any evidence of that happening. Rugby men are not angels, far from it. But after a hard training session or a hard game I doubt if they'd have enough energy to tackle anything other than a can of beer and bed. At least that's what Colin always tells me and who am I to argue?

Attitudes within the SRU have changed dramatically over the past ten years. In those days there was a sort of "them and us" atmosphere. The wives of players and those of committee members just didn't mix, and it's no joke hanging around waiting for your

The Deans family at home.

husband or boyfriend to join you after the official celebrations at the end of each match. I am not blaming the committee wives of those days. It was just one of those situations where I don't think either group really took the trouble to find out much about the other. So I'm delighted with the progress made although, like every woman, I can see some room for improvement yet. I think the players' wives should be asked along to ALL the functions attended by the committee members' spouses. That way what is at the moment a happy rugby ship — look at the improvement in results for the past few years — could be even happier and more effective. If a player knows his wife or girlfriend is being treated with fairness and courtesy it relieves his mind and lets him get on with the game.

I have only one tip for girls who wed rugby men with a burning ambition to get to the top — prepare to sacrifice a lot of your own life. Always remember that a sportsman's spell at the top is, comparatively speaking, a brief one and if he's doing well then he deserves his wife to give him encouragement.

I've been lucky with a husband like Colin. He's no macho man off the field but a gentle husband and superb father. But I knew what I was going in for long before we married. When we were courting, we had gone out for a walk and he poured out to me how it was his great ambition to get into the Hawick team like his dad, then hopefully make the grade to the South District side and ultimately a 'B' cap and the Scottish XV. He wasn't quite 18 then but I thought to myself, what a determined lad you are, and I never had the faintest doubt that he would make it to the top.

But it was hard on me at times. Even on our wedding day he whispered to me that he had received a letter from the SRU asking him to play for a Select XV in Holland and he wondered if we could postpone our honeymoon. Of course I said, "No." But I'm still looking forward to the honeymoon!

The first reasonably long tour Colin was involved with was to Japan and as there were only the two of us at the time I felt shattered once he had gone off with the boys. Fortunately my sister lives in Hawick and she insisted I stay with her. She had a young family so it helped keep my mind off things.

I remember the day Colin was due back. I was down at our own house cleaning and dusting from top to bottom, now and again peeking through the curtains to see if he had arrived. At last I heard the sound of a car and there, with his kitbag over his shoulder and that grin on his face, he smiled up at me.

My worst experience was when we had our second wee boy and again Colin was on tour, this time in New Zealand with the British Lions for 12 weeks. Three weeks into the tour wee Ross was born. It was a difficult birth and I don't think I've ever felt so lonely in my life. If rugby has left any scars on my heart, it was because of that experience of being alone when I most needed Colin.

I'm not going to kid you that everything is always sweetness and light. When you're coping with two wee boys and the big boy comes in with muddy, wet training clothes which have to be washed and ironed so that they are ready to be filthy again in a couple of nights' time, you begin to wonder if you've made the right choice. But it's like everything else in this life. You have a partnership and I think I've got a good partner in Colin. Even now when I see him on the field at Mansfield Park or Murrayfield my heart lifts, for there's no better sight than to see 15 young men going out without thought of reward to do their best for club or country.

I'm proud to have been involved in a minor way with Scottish rugby, even if it has only been to make sure the jerseys and stockings are clean. There are lots of golf widows who get their husbands back intact after a round or two. Rugby widows are a more exclusive club and a little knowledge of first aid is always useful. I still prefer the latter.